Blood of Freedom

Williamsburg in America Series

III

The third in a series of popular histories of Williamsburg and Tidewater Virginia in the eighteenth century.

BLOOD OF FREEDOM

The Story of Jamestown, Williamsburg, and Yorktown

BY

EARL SCHENCK MIERS

Published by
COLONIAL WILLIAMSBURG
WILLIAMSBURG, VIRGINIA

Distributed by Henry Holt and Company, Inc.
NEW YORK

Library of Congress Catalogue Card Number 58-13521

Printed in the United States of America

For

Holmes S. Wyckoff

Introductory Remarks

"THE earth," Thomas Jefferson said, "belongs always to the living generation." The modern American, visiting Jamestown, Williamsburg and Yorktown, does not step back through history. Rather, he brings to these shrines his own needs, his own attitudes, even his own conception of what patriotism truly is. What he sees with his eye and perceives with his heart is in itself an integral part of the continuing story. The visitor is an actor rather than a spectator in history; he is the human impulse of another generation receiving impressions and sensations that, becoming part of his own personality, constitute the modern force of American history. A generation hence—ten generations and more from now—the visitor may bring other needs and interests, other attitudes and aspirations as he explores these hallowed sites. On the breeze along the James, down Duke of Gloucester Street, above the bluffs at Yorktown he well may hear again the whisper of Jefferson's voice saying, "Nothing is unchangeable but the inherent and inalienable rights of man."

In the long span of years that begins on a bleak December day in 1606 at a Blackwall dock in London and ends in the bright sunshine of an October afternoon in 1781 on Surrender Field in Yorktown no truth has more significance than the fact that the people changed and the ideal endured. The fortune-seekers who stayed at Jamestown to build an empire, the great representative men of Williamsburg who were molded into patriots by a decade of crisis, the foot-weary soldiers who followed a valiant leader to victory on the battlefield at Yorktown, each in his way, and within his generation, reshaped his life to fit a principle that was no less a force then than it is now. Because so much of mind and heart and spirit became forged into the ideal, it became a living thing, the dominant human impulse that, wearing many faces and serving many ambitions, linked each of these three chapters into one story.

The objective of this book is to suggest how this impulse grew. Its purpose is not to explore all events or all the personalities who took part, for the physical limits of the work prohibit that undertaking. In large measure the actors in this drama have been allowed to tell their own story in their own language, and in their conceits, their pettiness, their self-interests, their confessions of fear and jealousy are much of essential history. For parents who today suffer the teaching of spelling to their children the prose of the 17th and 18th century should pose no great problem. The mind spoke to the ear, then and now. And the heart spoke to the mind, which was and still is the essence of the American story. To the members of the staff of Colonial Williamsburg who gave so cheerfully of their time, wisdom and skill to this book must go the commendation for what virtue it claims. Without exception its shortcomings belong to the author.

E. S. M.

Contents

JAMESTOWN

Doorway to Empire

CHESAPEAKE
BAY
Potomac River
Rappahannock River
Mattaponi River
Pamunkey River
Chickahominy River
York River
Gloucester
James River
Powhatan
Paspahegh
Henrico
Charles City
Middle Plantation
Archer's Hope
Martins Brandon
Appomattox River
JAMESTOWN
Hog Island
James River
Point Comfort
Cape Charles
Cape Henry
Hampton Roads
ATLANTIC OCEAN
THE LAND OF VIRGINIA
& Jamestown
1607 – 1619
0
10
20 Mi.

1

A Blazing Star

CHILL and fog along the Thames on a late December day in 1606 reminded prudent Londoners it was the season for bundling up in shawls and capes. In this age when England was changing from feudalism to capitalism, a Briton who couldn't adjust to adversity didn't deserve his mutton chop. Unhappily tradition, position, even merit did not always determine any more how well a man might live. An emerging industrialism has caused dislocations everywhere—for upper-class gentlemen, harder pinched from year to year to make their estates support them; for the laboring and middle classes, growing restless under rising unemployment. A few of course grew richer, and, rather like fussing hens, fretted over how to hatch the golden eggs piling up in their nests. "Help thyself, and God will help thee," said an aphorism of the age, reflecting that spirit of robust individualism that produced a Drake, a Raleigh or a Frobisher, and gave literature a Shakespeare.

At a Blackwall dock that late December day in 1606

gathered those two segments in England who, rolling with the punches fate would deal them, were willing to risk a shilling to make a pound or a neck to insure a brighter future. As hard-headed business men with eyes on a profit, the investors in the newly organized Virginia Company of London gazed proudly at the ships they had equipped to exploit their royal patent to all of the land of North America south of latitude 38. The *Susan Constant,* one hundred tons, looked sound in every timber; the *Godspeed,* forty tons, and even the *Discovery,* a pinnace of twenty tons, seemed trim and seaworthy. In ships such as these, trading adventures to Muscovy, the Levant, Guinea, India had paid off prettily; but the promise of the New World defied imagination. Last year, attending a play called *Eastward Ho!,* Londoners had listened to a hero who spoke the new dream:

"I tell thee golde is more plentifull in Virginia than copper is with us, and for as much redde copper as I can bring, I will have thrice the weight in gold. All their dripping pans and chamber potts are pure gould . . . and for rubies and diamonds, they goe forth in holidays and gather them by the seashore to hang on their children's coates and sticke in their children's caps. . . ."

A basis of reality supported the vision. Nothing had been more influential in toppling the old economy of Europe than the influx of gold from New Spain; and ever since the defeat of the Spanish Armada when "God blew and they scattered," England's palm had itched to deal itself into this game. The colony that Raleigh had planted (and lost) on Roanoke Island counted only as a temporary setback; the investors of the Virginia Company had placed aboard the *Susan Constant* two goldsmiths, two refiners, and a jeweler. If the gold were there, they meant to have it. With equal tenacity, they clung to a still older dream—somewhere in the New World, up this river or down that, existed a passage to the South Sea and the riches of the East.

Aboard the little fleet under the command of the experienced mariner, Captain Christopher Newport, the hearts of the passengers beat with these high hopes. In personality they differed from Captain John Smith, whose gusty tales of adventure stretched even a child's credulity, to Edward Brookes, Gentleman, who would pay a fearful forfeit for his corpulence. Captain Bartholomew Gosnold, commanding the *Godspeed,* two years before had explored the islands and bays off Cape Cod; John Laydon, carpenter, would wed a maidservant in the first English marriage ceremony on Virginia soil; and Master George Percy, eighth son of Henry, eighth earl of Northumberland, would publish *Observations* of the Virginia adventure that make it an Arabian Night's tale.

So had they come together, drawn by varying circumstances, each possessing his own good reason for being there. If too few were accomplished in crafts or hardened to labor, on the twentieth of December, 1606, as the ships at Blackwall dock cast loose their moorings and started down the Thames, they seemed a practical choice. By the fifth of January they reached the Kentish seacoast and the Downs, thanking God for the Goodwin Sands protecting them from an ocean tossed by wind and storm. Yet ultimately even British weather exhausts its passion; and at last began the voyage, longer, harder, more tedious, more exhausting on their bodies and supplies than any could have foreseen. Not until February twelfth did Percy observe an incident worth recording. That night he saw a blazing star.

On "the three and twentieth day [of March]," as the sun burned through the mists of the West Indies, the voyagers from the Old World beheld the land of the New. From Martinique they sailed to Dominica, a fair country of sweet scents and long-haired Indians with beardless faces and tattooed bodies who were Devil-worshippers. "They are continually in warres," Percy recorded, "and will eate their enemies when they kill them, or any stranger if they take them." Other habits revealed a people who existed "in a barbarous fashion like Dogges." Yet in this strange world, as the days passed, the voyage grew into an odyssey. For two hours they watched a whale fighting a thresher and a swordfish. At Marie Galente, a French possession, they found a hot spring, and, almost like adventuresome boys, boiled a piece of pork in it.

They passed Montserrat and St. Christopher, for both islands appeared uninhabited, then encamped six days on Nevis, believing the time well spent to throw off the diseases that a long voyage produced. To Percy's relief, the fear-stricken Indians "would not come to us by any meanes, but ranne swiftly through the Woods to the Mountaine tops." Resting and bathing, hunting and fishing, exploring the marvels of nature in this pinpoint paradise, they forgot the aching weariness of weeks at sea. At the Virgin Islands they anchored in a bay that could have harbored a hundred ships. "If this Bay stood in England," wrote Percy, reflecting the spirit of the times, "it would be a great profit and commoditie to the Land." Ashore on Porto Rico they killed wild boars and iguanas with speckled bellies, but this rough, steaming country caused many to faint and brought death to "one Edward Brookes Gentleman, whose fat melted within him."

Mid-April found the voyagers crossing the Tropic of Cancer. Again storms brought delay—an old story at sea now—and all one night, with sails furled, the ships rocked in the "winds, raine, and thunders" of a tempest. But on April twenty-sixth, toward four o'clock in the morning, Percy chronicled in triumph: "wee descried the Land of Virginia." Entering Chesapeake Bay "without any let or hinderance," Percy went ashore with a small party but "could find nothing worth the speaking of, but faire meddowes and goodly tall Trees, with such Fresh-waters running through the woods, as I was almost ravished at the first sight thereof." That afternoon when the explorers were returning to the boats the Indians attacked—"creeping upon all foure, from the Hills, like Beares, with their Bowes in their mouthes." Captain Gabriel Archer was "hurt" on both hands, a sailor twice wounded in the body, but "after they had spent their Arrowes, and felt the sharpnesse of our shot, they retired into the Woods with a great noise." Then it was night and the ships from the Old World rode quietly at anchor. Beyond those capes that would be named Charles and Henry stretched the tempest-ridden highway home. And ahead, beneath the stars, in a land of mystery and hostility, rested hazard and hope.

April ends, May begins. Each day the incredible becomes commonplace—great rivers awaiting discovery; beaches where mussels and oysters "lay on the ground as thicke as stones"; strawberries "foure times bigger and better then ours in England." Curiosity like love seems to level all ranks and in an old Indian town at the mouth of the Hampton Creek white men and savages feast on a bread of corn and wheat, sitting side by side on mats, cross-legged. The bodies of the Indians are smeared with black and red clays, and Percy, remarking that "they goe altogether naked, but their privities are covered," adds a note of London respectability to wilderness innocence. A group of Indians comes forward in a dance of welcome with "one of the Savages standing in the midst singing, beating one hand against another, all the rest dancing about him, shouting, howling, and stamping against the ground, with many Anticke tricks and faces, making noise like so many Wolves or Devils."

What the eyes see the mind must believe. A few days later, visiting the Paspaheghes along the north bank of the James, Percy gawks at a sachem who greets them "playing on a Flute made of a Reed, with a Crown of Deares haire colloured red, in fashion of a Rose fastened about his knot of haire, and a great Plate of Copper on the other side of his head, with two long Feathers in fashion of a paire of Hornes placed in the midst of his Crowne." The body of the sachem is painted crimson, beads hang around his neck, his face is stained blue, bracelets of pearls are suspended from earlobes in which are set bird claws decorated with copper and gold. On May eighth the white men explore the Indian lands in the region of the Appomattox River, and savages with bows and arrows, swords beset with sharp stones and pieces of iron "able to cleave a man in sunder" stand ready to repel the invaders. The chief advances, standing before them "cross-legged" and demands of us "to be gone." But the white men make signs of peace and are permitted to land "in quietnesse."

Four days later they explore a point of land made by the creek that starts about five miles inland near present-day Williamsburg. They call the place Archer's Hope and believe it could be easily defended. The soil looks "good and fruitfull," the timber excellent, and vines as big as a man's thigh run to the tree tops. Squirrels race across the ground and up the trees, chattering sassily; wings of crimson, pale blue, and dark red fill the air with brilliant flashes; every step threatens another nest of turkey eggs. "If it had not beene disliked, because the ship could not ride neere the shoare," Percy says, seeming to hide his own regret, "we had setled there to all the Collonies contentment." Next day, May thirteenth, a "seating place" is selected for a practical reason: "our shippes doe lie so neere the shoare that they are moored to the Trees in six fathom water." In honor of that thrifty Scot who occupied the throne of England, early narratives call the settlement James Fort, James Towne, and James Citty.

With good sense, the white men began at once to build a fort. That first night Indians on the river were frightened away, but with daylight another pair appeared, announcing that their sachem was coming and "would be merry with us with a fat Deare." On the eighteenth the chief arrived, accompanied by a hundred armed men. He made "great signes" for the settlers to lay their arms aside, and might have spared himself the trouble; yet if the sachem were offended he swallowed his pride and offered the white men as much land as they wanted. Then an Indian was detected stealing a hatchet in the fort. There was little ceremony in the manner in which the implement was wrested from him; a second Indian, seeing his comrade bested, dashed at the white man with a wooden sword, "thinking to beat out his braines." The settlers took up their guns and the sachem departed "in great anger," ending the jolly little affair. But two days later he sent over the deer, with forty men to carry it; they came, Percy declared, "more in villanie than any love they bare us." For sport, a target was set up and an Indian invited to try his bow on it. The fellow responded calmly, shooting the target a foot through; Percy could not disguise his discomfiture "being that a Pistoll could not pierce it." Next a steel target was tried and the arrow shattered. The Indian pulled out another arrow and bit it in his teeth. He seemed, Percy added somewhat needlessly, "to bee in a great rage."

One day along the James—"one of the famousest Rivers that ever was found by any Christian"—Percy saw "a Savage Boy about the age of ten yeeres" with "a head of haire of a perfect yellow and a reasonable white skinne, which is a Miracle amongst all Savages." Whether the lad was a descendant of the lost colony of Roanoke can be no more than a romantic conjecture. To Percy the boy became simply another wonder to place beside the great woods of beech, oak, cedar, cypress, walnut, and sassafras, the flowers spreading blankets of color upon every slope, the profusion of strawberries, mulberries, raspberries and other fruits, the rivers teeming with fish, the lush meadows, the deer, bears, foxes, otters, beavers, muskrats, "and wild beasts unknowne." From day to day, as knowledge of Indian manners and customs increased, Percy learned that "when they swere by their God which is the Sunne, no Christian will keep their Oath better." Each rising and setting of the sun was a period of devotion; then the Indians lifted hands and eyes to the sun and sprinkled on the ground a circle of dried tobacco; thus "they began to pray, making many Devillish gestures with a Hellish noise, foming at the mouth, staring with their eyes, wagging their heads and hands in such a fashion and deformitie as it was monstrous to behold."

Hunting and war were pleasure and duty to the Indian male; all the domestic drudgery fell to the women. Yet an Indian woman turned cheerfully to her tasks, mixing her flour with hot water until it became a paste she could shape, scalding it in boiling water until "it is sod thoroughly," then laying it on a smooth stone to bake in the sun. These tattooed ladies—brightly colored images of fowl, fish and animals covered their bodies—wore their hair all one length if they were married, and if maidens shaved the forepart and sides of their heads. The incredible stamina of these people was exemplified by an old fellow "above eight score yeeres of age," eyes sunken in his head, not a tooth in his gums, hair gray and beard "as white as any snow" (a miracle to Percy, who never before had heard of an Indian with hair on his face). "This Savage was as lusty and went as fast as any of us," recorded Percy with obvious envy.

Percy's *Observations* yield no clue to the bickering behind the scenes at Jamestown, and Captain John Smith, the core of the controversy, was neither objective nor impartial on the subject. History poses fewer problems more complex than getting at the truth about Smith; he is rogue or hero, imposter or prophet, depending on the credence given to his own accounts of an astonishing career. His life starts humbly in Lincolnshire, England, when in January, 1580, he is the first son born to tenants on the manor of Lord Willoughby. Apprenticed to a trade at the age of fifteen, his spirit chafes under this drudgery and off he runs to fight in the Netherlands and elsewhere. A lad who, obviously, possessed a rare flair for getting in and out of trouble, he captures a thief, is thrown overboard, is stranded on an uninhabited island and rescued, engages in a desperate sea-fight, and, rather getting the hang of the business, plans and wins battles.

Under Baron Kisell and now a captain, Smith hurries to Hungary and Transylvania where there are Turks to fight; and here his skill at ridding the world of infidels prompts a grateful prince to offer him a patent of nobility and a pension. Then luck deserts him—left for dead on a battlefield, he falls into the hands of the enemy and is taken to Constantinople to become a slave. From prince to pauper in virtually a wink might have discouraged others, but Smith has won the love of the wife of a Turkish pasha, and she intercedes for him with her brother, a pasha on the Sea of Azov. This rascal provides short comfort, making Smith a thresher on one of his granges and beating and reviling him at every chance; Smith seizes "his threshing bat, for they have no flailes," knocks out the fellow's brains, and, donning the dead man's clothes, escapes across the desert to a Russian garrison. Thereafter he travels throughout Europe, tries to take a hand in a war in Barbary, and returns to England in time for Captain Gosnold to persuade him to join the voyage to Virginia. He is signed as a planter.

Patient historians find many factual discrepancies in these romantic tales; and to the more critical Smith's writings tend to reaffirm the maxim that clever liars give details, but the cleverest don't. Smith held a good opinion of himself and scornfully denounced those who opposed him, yet the violence of his hatred becomes a virtue. He is no hypocrite; posterity knows precisely where he stands. At Jamestown, by Smith's account, all the trouble that befell him arose from others "envying his repute." By the time the voyagers reached Dominica nerves doubtless were frayed and tempers edgy. Here upon what Smith termed "scandalous suggestions"—that he intended to murder the members of the Council and make himself king—he was taken prisoner. His confederates, said the charges, were dispersed on all three ships, making him a thorough villain. Not until the night of April twenty-sixth, however, when for the first time the ships anchored in Chesapeake Bay, was the box containing the orders given in London for the management of the colony unsealed. Smith's name was among the seven appointed to a Council empowered to elect its own president. When after settling at Jamestown the Council was sworn in and Edward Maria Wingfield chosen president, the man whose name dominates all others in the legend of planting the first permanent English colony in America was still a prisoner and excluded from the meeting.

Through the busy days that followed Smith nursed his grudge. Work on the fort, the felling of trees to make a place for pitching tents, the cutting of clapboard to load on the ships, the planting of gardens, the visits from the Indians—through it all Smith's scowl lengthened, his resentment deepened. "The Precidents overweening jealousie," he wrote, bitter in the memory, "would admit no exercise at armes, or fortification but the boughs of trees cast together in the forme of a halfe moone by the extraordinary paines and diligence of Captaine Kendall." When Newport led a party to discover the head of the river, Smith went along—perhaps for the good reason that Wingfield wanted a rest from his petulance. In six days the party reached Powhatan's town, a pleasant place of twelve houses situated on a hill; they discovered the falls of the James; and Newport grew so entranced by dirt glimmering with yellow flecks that he carted a load of it home to England before anyone could tell him that it contained worthless pieces of mica. If on returning to Jamestown Smith expected to discover that Wingfield had managed to get the place into a thorough mess, he was not disappointed. He arrived to find "17 men hurt, and a boy slaine by the Salvages" and—the captain rarely failed to create the impression that, with God's help, he had appeared in the nick of time—"had it not chanced a crosse barre shot from the ships strooke down a bough from a tree amongst them, that caused them to retire, our men had all been slaine." Wingfield at last "was contented" to build a sensible fort, for Smith a subtle dig.

A month and two days after the ships had moored to the trees along the river's edge, James Fort was completed. The triangular bastion faced river, woods and swamp; at each corner a bulwark, shaped like a half moon, mounted formidable demiculverins. On June twentieth, after thirteen weeks, Smith's status as a "prisoner" ended and he was admitted to the Council. The time neared for the ships to return to London, and among the one hundred and four who would remain a spirit of letting bygones be bygones likely prevailed. But the vanity of John Smith, once ruffled, kept its porcupinish character:

> . . . they pretended, out of their commisserations, [he wrote, not hiding his sneer] to referre him to the Councell in England, to receave a check, rather then by particulating his designes, [and] make him so odious to the world, as to touch his life, or utterly overthrowe his reputation. But he much scorned their charitie, and publikely defied the uttermost of their crueltie. Hee wisely prevented their pollicies, though could not suppresse their envies; yet so wel he demeaned himselfe in this business, as all the company did see his innocencie, and his adversaries malice; and those suborned to accuse him, accused his accusers of subornation. Many untruthes were alleaged against him, but being so apparently disproved begat a generall hatred in the harts of the company against such unjust commanders. Many were the mischiefes that daily sprong from their ignorant (yet ambitious) spirits; but the good doctrine and exhortation of our preacher Mr Hunt reconciled them . . .

With Smith restored to grace, next day the colony was given communion; and on the twenty-second, with good news from the Indians that they "voluntarily desired peace," Newport started home.

"There were never Englishmen," in Percy's estimation, "left . . . in such miserie as wee were in this new discovered Virginia"; and Thomas Studley, the company's general keeper of the stores, recorded that "within tenne daies, scarse ten amongst us coulde either goe, or well stand, such extreame weaknes and sicknes oppressed us." At this circumstance, declared Studley, "none need mervaile"; with the ships gone "there remained neither taverne, beere-house, nor place of relife but the common kettell"; moreover, "had we beene as free from all sinnes as gluttony and drunkenness, we might have bin canonized for Saints." For all that Wingfield had served as a brave and distinguished soldier in the Lowlands, Studley joined in the favorite Jamestown sport of libeling his character, declaring that to such saintliness "our President would never have bin admitted." The charge that Wingfield reserved supplies for his own use the president indignantly denied; in late August, for the best of reasons, this argument between Studley and Wingfield stopped abruptly. Studley was dead.

Percy, a less biased witness, told a story equally grim: John Asbie dead of "the bloudie Flixe" (i.e., bloody flux or dysentery) on the sixth of August; George "Flowre" on the ninth "of the swelling"; William "Bruster," gentleman, on the tenth "of a wound given by the Savages."

Three died on the fourteenth, two on the fifteenth, one on the sixteenth, another next day, two again on the eighteenth, another on the nineteenth. On the twenty-second Captain Gosnold died and was buried with military honors. Before the month ended Percy had five more deaths to record; September began no more cheerfully, and Percy commented sadly: "Our men were destroyed with cruell diseases, as Swellings, Flixes, Burning Fevers, and by warres, and some departed suddenly, but for the most part they died of meere famine."

With Gosnold's death the bitter wrangling within the Council intensified. Wingfield's prudence in ordering supplies like sherry and brandy sealed up for emergencies pleased no one. "Lord," he wrote, knowing as well as Studley that his fellow colonists would never be canonized as saints, "how they then longed for to supp up that litle remnant, for they had nowe emptied all their owne bottles and all other that they could smell out." Smith rallied his forces against Wingfield and on the tenth of September this much maligned man was deposed; now John Ratcliffe became president, and Smith believed that peace had been restored, which was missing the mark by a wide margin. Whatever triumph Smith felt in this intrigue, Percy hardly shared. Life for him remained utterly abject:

> . . . Wee watched every three nights, lying on the bare cold ground, what weather soever came, [and] warded all the next day, which brought our men to

> bee most feeble wretches. Our food was but a small Can of Barlie sod in water, to five men a day, our drinke cold water taken out of the River, which was at a floud verie salt, at a low tide full of slime and filth, which was the destruction of many of our men. Thus we lived for the space of five moneths in this miserable distresse, not having five able men to man our Bulwarkes upon any occasion. . . .

If as the morning sun spread its rays along the James these wretched people remembered that only hours before the same sun had passed over London and Blackwall dock, none could blame those who cursed the day they ever heard of Virginia. They had come as seekers of fortune rather than as colonists. The dream of their age had become a will-o'-the-wisp, coaxing them across wild seas to this wretched loneliness in a wilderness that could swallow them up as relentlessly as it had wiped out every trace of the poor devils at Roanoke.

2

The Prophecy

A MIRACLE occurred. "If it had not pleased God to have put a terrour in the Savages hearts," Percy said, all would have been killed by "those vild and cruell Pagans." Any suggestion that compassion could move a childlike people, offering their tobacco each dawn and eventide to their sun god, could have no place in the canons of the Church of England; and there was not a poet at Jamestown to comprehend the epic they were living.

Yet with bread and corn, with fish and meat, the Indians came. "We were frequented by divers Kings in the Countrie," wrote Percy, revealing how widely the news of distress spread and hearts responded. On the eighteenth of September Ellis Kinistone [Kingston?] "starved to death with cold," and that night Richard Simmons died; next day Thomas Mouton perished, but generally the enfeebled grew stronger, the pinched lines of famine faded from face and body. Cooler weather swept away the maladies that had clung to every breeze creeping up from the marshes and swamps surrounding the settlement. Overhead wild ducks honked.

But reviving health stirred anew undercurrents of jealousy, distrust, and intrigue. Perhaps the raw memory of suffering and fear turned heads and clouded reason. Perhaps the terrible isolation of the place, a sense of having been abandoned, broke spirits and shattered faith. The Indians began to drift away. Under all faults an eminently practical man, John Smith emerged as a forceful leader, aggressive in his denunciation of those content to exist "from hand to mouth," understanding how much the doom and despair was their own creation.

Smith worked. At twenty-seven a man of vigor and energy, he put muscle behind his ideas. Yet his foraging trips for provisions into the newly discovered country of the Chickahominy left the fort unattended. The *Proceedings* of the colony, probably written by Anas Todkill after the death of Studley, picture Wingfield and Captain Kendall plotting with "sailers and other confederates" to seize a pinnace and head across the seas for England. Returning unexpectedly, Smith turns a small cannon on the ship, demanding that the party "stay or sinke in the river." Kendall is shot.

So began December, not yet a year since leaving London. "These brawles are so disgustfull, as some will say they were better forgotten," commented Todkill, plunging into still another plot, allegedly involving "The President and captaine Archer"—and again the scheme is "curbed" by Smith. But the approaching winter had its cheerful note. "The rivers," reported Todkill, a twinkle in his eye, "became so covered with swans, geese, duckes, and cranes, that we daily feasted with good bread, Virginia pease, pumpions, and putchamins, fish, fowle, and diverse sorts of wild beasts as fat as we could eat them: so that none of our Tuftaffaty [silken-dressed] humorists desired to goe for England."

John Smith would not break. In this youthful, strong-willed man there must have been some trace of those fair-skinned, red-haired Celts who, centuries before, had dug into Wales and the Scottish Highlands, determined to endure. His strong passions were supported by stronger sense; the legends he wrote were no more stirring than the one he now lived. He was force and purpose, insight and direction in a wilderness where the rainbow had led to grief and disillusionment. If, as he said, Powhatan ordered him seized and Pocahontas saved his life, then he had received another sign that God favored him. That belief had created Jamestown; that belief must keep it going through discouragements beyond imagination.

By April, 1609, he has set the colony on its feet—a glassworks produces "a trail of glasse"; a well yields "excellent sweete water"; some twenty houses have been built and the church re-covered; fishing nets dry on the river bank;

a blockhouse on the neck of the island guards against thieving Indians; at least thirty acres have been planted; pigs root in the streets, chickens peck and cackle. In 1608, and again in 1609, ships come from England, bringing fresh supplies, more settlers, and the population of Jamestown approaches five hundred. If the dreams of quick riches from gold and discovery of a passage to the South Sea fade, by Smith's standards it does not matter. Sweat and toil, wit and faith—these are his resources. The second winter, once more facing starvation, he divides the settlers into three parties to search for food. He is a colonizer, a shadow in the wilderness which can lengthen into the image of empire. At home and in the colony his enemies are sharp in their abuse of his administration and high-handed treatment of the Indians; they demand his resignation, clearly not understanding the futility of threats on such a man. Then he is dangerously wounded in a gunpowder explosion and returns to England. Within weeks Jamestown falls apart.

But not for that fact alone. From Plymouth on June 2, 1609, a fleet of seven ships and two pinnaces set sail for Virginia. The capable leader of this Third Supply, numbering more than four hundred new colonists, was Sir Thomas Gates, who had been knighted for his services in the wars of the Low Countries and now was to become governor and deputy for Lord Delaware in Virginia. The admiral of the fleet was Sir George Somers, a seasoned mariner; the vice-admiral was Captain Christopher Newport, who had helped to bring the first settlers to Jamestown. The admiral's vessel, usually called *Sea Venture* although some accounts give the name as *Sea Adventure,* ignored the route hitherto taken through the West Indies and headed straight for Virginia. Good fortune favored the voyagers until they were within seven or eight days of Cape Henry when, in the stark words of Captain Gabriel Archer, the fleet plunged into "a most terrible and vehement storme, which was a taile of the West Indian Horacano." The ships wallowed in wind-swept seas, and, Archer recounted, "men could scarce stand upon the Deckes, neither could any man heare another speake." There could be no choice: "Every man steered his owne course." Yet, remarkably, the tempest drove most of the ships toward Virginia so that in time all of the voyagers except the official party aboard the flagship limped to anchorage at Jamestown. Meanwhile for the *Sea Venture,* blown off course and smashing aground on one of the islands in the "still-vexed Bermoothes," a miracle of the sea unfolded.

Aboard the flagship with Gates and Somers sailed William Strachey, occasional student at Cambridge, member of Gray's Inn, and a minor literary figure and shareholder in acting companies in the London of Shakespeare and Ben Jonson. Strachey was a representative son of those British families which, rising from yeomen to the fringes of the gentry, often fell upon days of indigence when a voyage to Virginia gave the best promise of a happier future. So sailed Strachey from Plymouth, full of hope; so lived Strachey through an adventure in the Bermudas that belonged in a saga; and in a letter to a "noble lady," probably the wife of the treasurer of the Virginia Company, Strachey gave an account of hurricane, disaster and its aftermath that, coming into the hands of Shakespeare, provided the background for *The Tempest.*

Indeed to Strachey, caught in a storm when "there was not a moment in which the sodaine splitting, or instant over-setting of the Shippe was not expected," it must have seemed as though a Prospero cast his evil spell. Rigging fell in shreds, seams opened, and yet, the first miracle, the full company struggled safely ashore. Eleven incredible months followed. In Gates and Somers—one the old soldier, the other an old seadog—was the iron will of men used to pitting duty against unreasonable adversity. While God gave them breath they intended to survive. The island provided food in abundance—fish, crabs, turtles, birds, eggs, hogs, palmetto cabbages. They had shelters erected, gardens planted. Ordering cedars cut and using what timbers could be salvaged from the *Sea Venture,* they set the castaways to building two new vessels. But there were those who refused to work, those who organized mutinous factions; and one Henry Paine, "after he had made many confessions," was sentenced to be hung.

Yet Strachey was not without feeling for the culprit: "hee earnestly desired, being a Gentleman, that hee might be shot to death, and towards the evening he had his desire, the Sunne and his life setting together." Strachey, a good teller of a story, understood essential details. These were green cedars with which the carpenters toiled; even craftsmen can become heroes. In nine months the new ships were completed, and with a sense for succinct history amounting to genius, one was named *Deliverance* and the other *Patience.*

In Bermuda, during these months, one catches a glimpse of John Rolfe and his bride. In no small measure the future of Virginia will depend on this modest man; now he is only one of the many faithful who labor. The child his wife carries is born and christened Bermuda; within a brief time the infant daughter has been buried and the incident has significance as part of a chain. So also do the hardship, the heartbreak, the exposure at sea when at last the voyage to Jamestown can be resumed, for each traces its mark on Mrs. Rolfe. She too will die soon after Gates and his party reach Virginia in May, 1610. Again the incident is part of a chain.

Meanwhile Jamestown had lived through the terrifying winter of 1609-10—"the starving time" when the suffering surpassed belief. For each settler who endured, nine perished. Those who had ridden out the tempest to reach the colony arrived with supplies spoiled so that they brought only more hungry mouths to feed. Despair moaned on the pestilent winds that swept across the surrounding swamps; fear grew into an oozing thing, like the brackish water from the river seeping into the well; even the imagination of a Milton or a Dante could not conceive of a hell worse than these dispirited, wretched people faced. George Percy watched the poor devils who had fed upon "horses and other beastes" as long as they lasted become "gladd to make shifte" on dogs, cats, rats, mice. Some who robbed the store, while such existed, were executed. Anything drawn up in the nets was eaten, along with boots or "any other leather." Men searched the woods, eager "to feede upon Serpents and snakes and to digge the earthe for wylde and unknowne Rootes." Here Indians stalked them, catching them alone, killing quickly, grinning at the screams. No one could describe the torment of Jamestown, Percy declared, unless he "hath Tasted the bitternesse thereof." Writing from hearsay, John Smith told of "one amongst the rest" who killed his wife, "powdered" or salted her, and had eaten part of the cache before he was discovered; the fellow was executed "as hee well deserved," Smith said, appending with bitter humor: "Now whether shee was better roasted, boyled or carbonado'd, I know not; but of such a dish as powdered wife I never heard of."

On the twentieth of May, toward midnight, as the *Deliverance* and *Patience* entered the James, Strachey remembered "a marvellous sweet smell from the shoare . . . strong and pleasant, which did not a little glad us." Daylight brought the terrible revelation of what had happened to Jamestown. By nature a straightforward man, Strachey stated the case simply: "Unto such calamity can sloath, riot, and vanity bring the most setled and plentifull estate." For a time Gates tried to surmount the despondency and fear, the black and evil memories that haunted the sixty survivors, but early in June Gates admitted that hopelessness had won and the cause of the little colony seemed all but lost. Wherever Gates turned he heard the same sullen mutter: what remained of Jamestown would be better burned to the ground. Let the houses stand, Gates argued—what did it matter as long as he agreed to take the survivors in quest of the fishing fleet off Newfoundland so that they could secure passage to England? In the *Deliverance,* the *Patience,* and two of the four pinnaces remaining at Jamestown, the settlers started down the James. At Hog Island, seven miles below the settlement, a longboat was sighted. Delaware had reached the colony with new supplies! His fleet already had dropped anchor in Hampton Roads! Gates and his party turned back to the scenes of dreaded memory, suspending the life and death of Jamestown upon that thin thread of coincidence.

Yet, understandably, in the months that followed on both sides of the Atlantic the discouragement deepened.

Listening to Gates and to Delaware who followed him to London, investors in the colony shook their heads. Throwing good money after bad—what else did Virginia represent now? But the courage of the old soldier in Gates, the streak of British stubbornness, prevailed. He had seen Jamestown at its worst, and yet he had seen too the vision that John Smith always had understood—that toil, patience, perseverance, faith, principle build colonies and empire. In August, 1611, Gates brought another six ships across the sea. Three hundred additional men came with him, one hundred head of cattle, all manner of provisions. Assuming office as governor, Gates set about rebuilding Jamestown with religion as the foundation of law and order. His administration was brief, yet Virginia, touched by the spirit of this man, became revitalized. A settlement was founded at Henrico, a third patent for the colony signed, and suddenly a resource of wealth discovered.

If thrift and obstinacy were among the traits in James I, events in Virginia soon demonstrated that this crafty Scot could take a profit and let a prejudice go. James liked the comfort of old shoes, old ideas, old habits; throughout England and Western Europe the use of tobacco had become a craze, and where others might attribute all sorts of health-giving properties to tobacco, saying it was good for everything from gunshot wounds to epilepsy, the king still despised the "filthie noveltie." In a pamphlet entitled

A Counterblaste to Tobacco he railed against this "custome lothsome to the eye, hatefull to the Nose, harmefull to the braine, dangerous to the Lungs, and in the blacke stinking fume thereof, neerest resembling the horrible Stigian smoke of the pit that is bottomelesse." Of an avid smoker who had died unexpectedly James claimed that the poor fellow's body, when opened, contained a bushel of soot! In time, however, James tended to forget this frightful example and if ever silence was golden, here was a case of it. Glassmaking, silk worms, timber, soap ashes, the medicinal uses of sassafras all had failed to produce a realistic economy for Virginia; then the cultivation of tobacco was introduced in 1612 and within seven years John Pory wrote home: "All our riches for the present doe consiste in Tobacco, wherein one man by his owne labour hath in one yeare raised to himselfe to the value of 200 £ [pounds] sterling; and another by meanes of sixe servants hath cleared at one crop a thousand pound English."

Behind this triumph stood the modest figure of John Rolfe, who had buried his baby in Bermuda and his wife in Virginia. Rolfe walked quietly into the history of Virginia, leading no one to suspect that he had been cast in the mold of an Homeric hero; sensitive and imaginative, he emerged as a symbol of many divisive forces at play between the Old World and the New. So in effect might he teach a king to hold his tongue on the subject of tobacco, but the essential drama was much more far-reaching than that. Again the seeds of conflict were so deeply hidden that centuries obscured their images, yet red-haired Celt and dark Iberian, Roman and Saxon and Norman had each produced in some measure the character and sentiments of these Englishmen in Virginia. Such interplay *was* history. The process was slow, indiscernible, tormenting; and again had there been a poet to relate the unfolding epic he might have sensed how much of this coming upheaval was focused in a single heart.

The nature of John Rolfe shines through the remark of a contemporary who watched him fussing over his tobacco—"Partly for the love he hath a long time borne unto it." Rolfe was both husband of the soil and experimenter, understanding that the tobacco native to Virginia possessed a strong, bitter taste and cultivating instead the sweeter varieties grown in the Caribbean and South America. In the simplicity of the idea rested Rolfe's genius; here was the crop that Europe wanted, so eagerly that the day would come at Jamestown when even the streets between the houses would be plowed up to grow the weed. Yet more than tobacco filled the eye and mind of John Rolfe. His courtship of the Indian princess, Pocahontas, was scarcely an idyll for this Old World lover surrounded by Old World neighbors with Old World notions and Old World tongues gifted in gossip.

In the agony of self-torture, Rolfe had to pour out his heart to someone.

Rarely does any man reveal so poignantly the suffering of heart and conscience as Rolfe did when in the spring of 1614 he wrote his letter to Sir Thomas Dale, now deputy governor of the colony. His ordeal, since first love for the Indian maid "began to roote it selfe within the secret bosome of my brest," Rolfe confesses with brutal candor. He addresses Dale "from an unspotted conscience," not unmindful of those "malicious depravers, and turbulent spirits, to whom nothing is tastful, but what pleaseth their unsavory pallat." Let their loose tongues wag—"in the undertaking of so mightie a matter" he can testify that he has not been led by "the unbridled desire of carnall affection." He has acted "for the good of this plantation, for the honour of our countrie, for the glory of God, for my owne salvation, and for the converting to the true knowledge of God and Jesus Christ, an unbeleeving creature, namely Pokahuntas."

So speaks John Rolfe, Englishman and Christian, whose "hartie and best thoughts are, and have for a long time bin so intangled, and inthralled in so intricate a laborinth, that I was even awearied to unwinde my selfe thereout." Cut to the quick by the malicious whisperings, he has pondered the fraility of mankind, its proneness to evil, its wickedness of mind, and the "many other imperfections wherein man is daily insnared." Nor is he ignorant of "the heavie displeasure which almightie God conceived against the sonnes of Levie and Israel for marrying strange wives." Time and again he has demanded of himself what "should provoke me to be in love with one whose education hath bin rude, her manners barbarous, her generation accursed." In "feare and trembling" he has thought: "Surely these are wicked instigations, hatched by him who seeketh and delighteth in mans destruction."

Daily, hourly, "yea and in my sleepe," Rolfe recounts his lonely debate—how he has awakened in astonishment, taxed with feelings of guilt and with "the duetie of a good Christian, pulling me by the eare, and crying: why dost not thou indevour to make her a Christian?" Asking "Why I was created?" he answers in a soliloquy that is enormously moving:

"What should I doe? shall I be of so untoward a disposition as to refuse to leade the blinde into the right way? Shall I be so unnaturall, as not to give bread to the hungrie? or uncharitable as not to cover the naked? Shall I despise to actuate the pious dueties of a Christian? Shall the base feare of displeasing the world, overpower and with holde mee from revealing unto man these spirituall workes of the Lord, which in my meditations and praiers, I have daily made knowne unto him? God forbid."

So in "the cleereness of my conscience," so knowing he was "clean from the filth of impurity," the man from the Old World would marry the savage princess from the New. Dale must have found the letter provocative, filling in between the lines as Rolfe snaps: "Now if the vulgar sort, who square all mens actions by the base rule of their own filthinesse, shall taxe or taunt me in this my godly labour: let them know, it is not any hungry appetite, to gorge my selfe with incontinency; sure (if I would, and were so sensually inclined) I might satisfie such desire, though not without a seared conscience, yet with Christians more pleasing to the eie, and lesse fearefull in the offence unlawfully committed." He has wrestled with pride too, for one day he would return to England where he was neither "so void of friends, nor mean in birth" that he could not there make a match to his "great content."

The first mention of Pocahontas brings this daughter of Powhatan to Jamestown in 1608 as a friendly emissary from her royal father. She is then a child of about thirteen, a little sprite who pleases the colonists with her capering and dancing, and John Smith, with an eye for noticing everything, remarked that for "feature, countenance, and proportion" she "much exceedeth" other Indians. *The Proceedings of the English Colony in Virginia* for 1609 record that the child has saved Smith's life, and "some propheticall spirit calculated hee had the Salvages in such subjection, hee would have made himselfe a king, by marrying Pocahontas." The child is "very oft" at the fort; her affection for Smith is known to everyone, and an intriguing sentence adds: "If he would, he might have married her, or have done what him listed; for there was none that could have hindred his determination."

Apparently wherever the sprightly goodness of an Ariel exists, the treachery of a Calaban must linger, and there is the dimension of comedy in the absurd plot that brings Pocahontas back to Jamestown in 1612. The villain is Sir Samuel Argall, who has not yet made himself thoroughly disliked by everyone. His scheme is to abduct Pocahontas, hold her aboard his pinnace and demand a pretty ransom from Powhatan, a bit of guileful calculation that had but one flaw—Powhatan's refusal to have any part of it. Argall admitted his defeat, and Rolfe, looking up from his tobacco plants, beheld the maid who at seventeen doubtless still deserved appreciation for "feature, countenance, and proportion." Pocahontas was baptized the following April, taking the Christian name of Rebecca, and next year she and Rolfe were married. She wore a tunic of white muslin over which hung a robe she had embroidered. A glittering band decked her forehead; feathers were fastened in her hair; she wore a white bridal veil. Powhatan sent his consent to the marriage by courier. Although Pocahontas was counted the favorite among his ten daughters, Powhatan's distrust for the white settlers outweighed that sentiment. He never visited Jamestown.

In England, John Rolfe and Lady Rebecca were received with great kindness and "La Belle Sauvage" became a favorite name of taverns. On the eve of returning to Virginia, Lady Rebecca was fatally stricken with an illness variously identified as smallpox, pneumonia or tuberculosis. Burying his wife at Gravesend and leaving their son Thomas to be raised and educated in England, Rolfe made the lonely voyage back to Jamestown. In later years Thomas came to Virginia, acquiring wealth and distinction as a planter of the tobacco his father had introduced; and through Thomas's daughter spring the Virginia families of Bolling, Fleming, Murray, Guy, Robertson, Whittle, Elbridge, and a branch of the Randolphs.

England's toehold in Virginia irked Spain. When in 1611 a Spanish caravel appeared in the James River and sent three of its passengers ashore at Point Comfort looking for a pilot, the trio were captured as spies. Five years elapsed before Dale consented to cart them back to Europe; by then Marco Antonio had died in Virginia and enroute another of the group, Francisco Lembri, was proved to be an English subject and executed as a traitor. About 1618 the surviving spy, Don Diego de Molina, managed to return to Spain, filled with enthusiasm for

Virginia and its reputed silver mine, alarmed that Spain would not move quickly enough to "stop the progress of a hydra in its infancy" that intended "to grow and encompass the destruction of all the West, as well by sea as by land," and dangling before the Spanish king an alluring vision of how easily he might pluck the plum of Virginia:

> . . . With eight hundred or one thousand soldiers he [the king] could reduce this place with great ease, or even with five hundred, because there is no expectation of aid from England for resistance and the forts which they have are of boards and so weak that a kick would break them down, and once arrived at the ramparts those without would have the advantage over those within because its beams and loopholes are common to both parts—a fortification without skill and made by unskilled men. . . .

The men, Molina insisted, were "poorly drilled and not prepared for military action"—he belonged to the old Spanish school whose contempt for the British curled like their mustachios. Where Spain hesitated in contesting with England for North America, France did not. In 1611 and again in 1613 Jesuit priests arrived to plant stations on Mt. Desert Island. Governor Dale sensed the threat to future English colonization in New England and hurried off an expedition under Argall to burn these settlements. Argall's martial gifts were many, those of diplomacy few.

As deputy Governor of Virginia from 1617 to 1619 his enactment of severe sumptuary laws and arbitrary conduct in general nettled everyone, and tears were sparse when at last he was recalled to England.

A golden year followed. The English were learning about colonization; there was a spirit that seemed to say if they were going to trouble with Virginia they should do the thing right—with boldness, with willingness to experiment, with faith in the future. So they talked of the need to secure "a fitt hundredth" of "woemen, Maides young and uncorrupt to make wifes to the Inhabitantes and by that meanes to make the men there more setled & lesse moveable." Men who came to Virginia simply "to gett something and then to returne for England," the backers of the Company now recognized, "will breed a dissolution, and so an overthrow of the Plantation." Never, declared the minutes of the Company for November, 1619, was there "fitter time to send them than nowe," and the following May and June the marriageable ladies arrived—at Company expense if they wedded "publiq Farmors," otherwise at the expense of their future husbands.

Without design 1619 cast a second long shadow across the future of Virginia and America when a Dutch man-of-war appeared at Point Comfort with "not any thing but 20. and odd Negroes, which [the letter is John Rolfe's] the Governor and Cape Marchant bought for victualles."

In settled family life, in tobacco and a plantation system with slaves to support it . . . thus the pattern of a new Virginia began to emerge, and yet still another event, constituting a revolution in the concept of English colonization, occurred that summer of 1619 in the choir of the church at Jamestown.

Sir George Yeardley, newly knighted by James I, a mild-mannered man certain to be popular after the struts and bluster of Argall, takes his seat as governor. Next to him, on either side, sit the members of the Council. The Speaker's chair is occupied by John Pory, who also serves as Secretary; beside him sits the clerk, John Twine, with Thomas Pierse, the sergeant, "standing at the barre, to be ready for any service." Two representatives are present from James Citty, Charles Citty, Henrico, Kiccowtan as Elizabeth City is then called, Brandon's plantation on the south side of the James, Smythe's Hundred running along the north side of the river from Weyanoke to the Chickahominy, Martin's Hundred in the east end of present James City County, Argall's Gift about a mile north of Jamestown, Flowerdieu Hundred on the south side of the James about midway between Brandon and City Point, Captain Lawne's plantation at Lawne's Creek in Isle of Wight County, and Captain Warde's plantation on the southside of the James above Brandon.

These are the scene, the people, the area of settlement

when on the thirtieth of July, 1619, the first legislative assembly in America convenes. The burgesses pray, then take an oath of allegiance to the king—with "none staggering at it," in Pory's happy phrase. Exception is taken to Captain Warde; he has settled on Martin's land and is "but a limbe or member of him"; both do not deserve delegates at the Assembly. Thus upon a principle of fair representation self-government in America starts. Martin also is called to answer a complaint against his men for using force to coerce the Indians to trade. "Suche outrages as this might breede danger and loss of life to others of the Colony," read the minutes, sounding a keynote that defines the essential purpose of self-government.

Attention turns to the instructions Yeardley has brought from England—"not to correcte or controll anything," but from their own insight into the life and necessities of the colony to judge if "any lawe . . . did presse or binde too harde, that we might by waye of humble petition, seeke to have it redressed, especially because this great Charter is to bind us and our heyers for ever." Six petitions are presented next day. A complete clarification of past land grants is requested, and the Company is asked to "allowe to the male children, of them and of all others begotten in Virginia, being the onely hope of a posterity, a single share a piece, and shares for their issues or for themselves, because that in a newe plantation it is not knowen whether man or woman be more necessary."

Appointment of a sub-treasurer to collect rents in the colony is urged as good sense; a request is made that "workmen of all sortes, fitt for that purpose" be sent to expedite construction of the proposed "University and Colledge"; and finally permission is sought "to change the savage name of Kiccowtan." In England Yeardley had been told to experiment with silk, iron and wine in an effort to reduce the colony's dependence on tobacco, but the burgesses are more realistic, knowing what butters their bread, and fix 3*s* a pound as the price for the best tobacco and 18*d* for "the second sorte."

On Sunday, August 1, the burgesses observe the Sabbath, and they have need for their spiritual refreshment for on Monday they determine laws affecting the general welfare of the colony. They are dealing, in substance, with human nature in a wilderness where to "know thyself" becomes the essence of their labors—specifically to know their own traits and passions and to protect themselves against what Rolfe had described as "wicked instigations, hatched by him who seeketh and delighteth in mans destruction." Thus they decree "that no injury or oppression be wrought by the English against the Indian whereby the present peace might be disturbed and antient quarrells might be revived"—they put the first fear first. Then in a series of decrees they look inwardly upon themselves:

First, in detestation of Idleness be it enacted, that if any man be founde to live as an Idler or renagate, though a freedman, it shalbe lawful for that Incorporation or Plantation to which he belongeth to appoint him a Mr [Master] to serve for wages, till he shewe apparant signes of amendment.

Against gaming at dice and Cardes be it ordained by this present assembly that the winner or winners shall lose all his or their winninges and both winners and loosers shall forfaite ten shillings a man, one ten shillings whereof to go to the discoverer, and the rest to charitable and pious uses in the Incorporation where the faulte is comitted.

Against drunkenness be it also decreed that if any private person be found culpable thereof, for the first time he is to be reprooved privately by the Minister, the second time publiquely, the thirde time to lye in boltes 12 howers in the house of the Provost Marshall and to paye his fee, and if he still continue in that vice, to undergo suche severe punishment as the Governor and Counsell of Estate shall thinke fitt to be inflicted on him. But if any officer offende in this crime, the first time he shall receive reprooff from the Governour, the second time he shall openly be reprooved in the churche by the minister, and the third time he shall first be comitted and then degraded. Provided it be understood that the Governor hath alwayes power to restore him when he shall in his discretion thinke fitte.

Against excesse in apparell that every man be cessed

> in the churche for all publique contributions, if he be unmarried according to his owne apparell, if he be married, according to his owne and his wives, or either of their apparell.

Another group of laws regulated personal relations with the Indians, for "the Assembly who knowe well their dispositions thinke it fitte to enjoin, least to counsell those of the Colony, neither utterly to reject them nor yet to drawe them to come in." Where in deer hunting, fishing, beating of corn or other work intercourse with Indians was maintained, no more than five or six should be admitted at any time in one place without the Governor's consent since "they are a most trecherous people and quickly gone when they have done a villany." They should be lodged apart for the same reason and "lone inhabitants" should by no means entertain them. Yet, looking to the future, the burgesses provided "that for laying a surer foundation of the conversion of the Indians to Christian Religion, eache towne, citty, Borrough, and particular plantation do obtaine unto themselves by just means a certine number of the natives' children to be educated by them in true religion and civile course of life—of which children the most towardly boyes in witt and graces of nature to be brought up by them in the first elements of litterature, so to be fitted for the Colledge intended for them that from thence they may be sente to that worke of conversion." Finally a set of laws provided for systematic cultivation of corn, mulberry trees, silk-flax, aniseed and vineyards and safeguarded against "crafty or advantagious means . . . for the inticing awaye the Tenants or Servants of any particular plantation from the place where they are seatted." Tobacco, however, remained the staff of life to the colony; all men are enjoined "thoroughly and loyally to aire their Tobacco before they bring it to the Magazine," and in cases of transgression "it shall there imediately be burnt before the owner's face."

Tuesday gave the assembly a fascinating break from lawmaking in the petition of Captain William Powell

> . . . against one Thomas Garnett, a servant of his, not onely for extreame neglect of his business to the great loss and prejudice of the said Captaine, and for openly and impudently abusing his house, in sight both of Master and Mistress, through wantonnes wth a woman servant of theirs, a widdowe, but also for falsely accusing him to the Governor both of Drunkennes and Thefte, and besides for bringing all his fellow servants to testifie on his side, wherein they justly failed him. . . .

That Garnett was ordered to stand four days in pillory should have surprised no one.

August dog days were beginning to tell, and on the fourth the Assembly determined to end its session that day with a consideration of "a thirde sorte of lawes (suche as might proceed out of every man's private conceipt)." No "English dog of quality" could be sold or given to an Indian nor could any man "sell or give any Indians any piece shott or poulder, or any other armes, offensive or defensive" except upon pain of being hung as a traitor. Indian towns or habitations could not be "purposely" visited without the governor's permission, nor could a man travel more than twenty miles from his dwelling-place or be absent more than seven days without the same permission. Likewise, he could kill no cattle whatsoever, young or old, without leave of the Governor. Anas Todkill once had observed that few at Jamestown ran risk of being canonized as saints, and other laws indicate that Todkill's judgment might still be valid:

> The Ministers and Churchwardens shall seeke to presente all ungodly disorders, the comitters wherofe if, upon goode admontions and milde reprooff, they will not forbeare the said skandalous offenses, as suspicions of whordomes, dishonest company keeping with weomen and suche like, they are to be presented and punished accordingly.

Excommunication from church and seizure of property could be applied to "enormous sinnes" and even swearing earned telling penalties—after three admonitions, a fine of 5*s* for a freeman, a public whipping for a servant. A law governing marriages provided that:

> No maide or woman servant, either now resident in the Colonie or hereafter to come, shall contract herselfe in marriage wthout either the consente of her parents, or of her Mr or Mris, or of the magistrate and minister of the place both together. And whatsoever minister shall marry or contracte any suche persons without some of the foresaid consentes shalbe subjecte to the severe censure of the Governor and Counsell of Estate.

When finally the work of the first Assembly was finished, it would leave a record filled with the story of a colony and a people who had come far in twelve years—so far, indeed, that with rare insight the record ends in prophecy: ". . . the General Assembly doth humbly beseech the said Treasurer, Counsell and Company . . . that it would please them not to take it in ill parte if these lawes which we have now brought to light, do passe currant and be of force till suche time as we may knowe their farther pleasure out of Englande: for otherwise this people (who nowe at length have gotten the raines of former servitude into their own swindge) would in shorte time growe so insolent, as they would shake off all government, and there would be no living among them."

3

Massacre and Rebellion

THE whisper of spring crept into the breeze that stirred the marsh grasses along the James early in March of 1622. On plantations that reached up the river more than sixty miles above Jamestown the colonists believed that they were learning how to survive in this wilderness. The speedy conversion of the Indians to Christianity had lessened one of their greatest tensions. To win the devotion of Opechancanough, the second successor of Powhatan, the settlers had built a "faire house after the English fashion" with a lock and key that so pleased this guileful fellow he was seen locking and unlocking his door a hundred times a day. The Englishman's "God was better than theirs," Opechancanough declared, knowing how to butter his bread. Throughout the Virginia settlements white men grew accustomed to Indians appearing in the fields or in the doorway at mealtime, and often the Indians were invited to eat at the same table with the settlers and "lodged in their bedchambers."

A disturbing incident occurred. An Indian called Jack of the Feather was much respected among his own people, to whom he boasted that he was "immortall from any hurt [that] could bee done him by the English." On a pleasant day in early March of 1622, appearing at the plantation of a settler named Morgan, Jack persuaded Morgan to accompany him on a trading trip. The circumstances that led Jack to murder Morgan are not explained; when some two or three days later Jack reappeared, wearing the white man's cap and stating only that the other was dead, two boys who were servants to Morgan found the explanation dissatisfying. The genius of John Smith's *Generall Historie of Virginia* is that a few words convey much; thus, in a sentence, the result was that "Jack so moved their patience, they shot him." They placed Jack in a boat, determined to sail the seven or eight miles down river and deliver him to the governor, but Jack, "finding the pangs of death upon him," begged that he be buried among the English and no one told that, after all, a bullet had proved him to be quite mortal. When news of Jack's death reached Opechancanough, the lock and key to his door were poor solace; he was "much grieved and repined, with great threats of revenge," to which "the English returned him . . . terrible answers," whereupon Opechancanough "cunningly dissembled his intent, with the greatest signes he could of love and peace."

During the next fortnight the childlike Opechancanough played his own quiet game with the childlike English, relying, in the tart phrase of Smith, on "the conceit of this conceited peace" derived from the belief that they were all Christians under the skin. "The sky should fall," declared a messenger from Opechancanough, before such a peace as theirs should be dissolved. The Indians, living in bands of thirty, forty or fifty so that they seemed to present no one concentrated menace, said one thing among themselves and another when they mingled with the English. With much kindness they continued to guide the settlers through the woods, and on the morning of Good Friday appeared in many places with turkeys, deer, fish, fruits and other provisions to sell. Many were invited to take breakfast with the colonists and accepted in convivial spirit; thus strengthened for their day's labors, they fell to the massacre they had been carefully plotting for two weeks.

Using what weapons or tools were about the houses, the Indians "slew most barbarously, not sparing either age or sex, man woman or childe." Fortunately, in most cases, the slaughter was completed so quickly "that few or none discerned the weapon or blow that brought them to destruction." With the same disarming friendliness the Indians appeared in the fields where the settlers worked. The massacre reached terrifying limits, for the savages, not content with neat and simple execution, "fell againe upon the dead bodies, making as well as they could a fresh murder, defacing, dragging, and mangling their dead carkases into many peeces, and carrying some parts away in derision, with base and brutish triumph."

The wild morning lives once more in the grim, spare language of Smith:

> ... Captaine Nathaniel Powell one of the first Planters, a valiant Souldier, and not any in the Countrey better knowne amongst them; yet such was the error of an overconceited power and prosperitie, and their simplicities, they not onely slew him and his family, but butcher-like hagled their bodies, and cut off his head, to expresse their uttermost height of cruelty. ... In one place, where there was but two men that had warning of it, [they] defended the house against sixty or more that assaulted it. ... they came to one Master Harisons house ... where was Master Thomas Hamer with six men, and eighteene or nineteene women and children. Here the Salvages with many presents and faire perswasions, fained they came for Capt. Ralfe Hamer to go to their King, then hunting in the woods: presently they sent to him, but he not comming as they expected, set fire of a Tobacco-house, and then came to tell them in the dwelling house of it to quench it; all the men ran towards it but Master Hamer, not suspecting any thing, whom the Salvages pursued, shot them full of arrowes, then beat out their braines. Hamer having finished a letter hee was a writing, followed after to see what was

> the matter, but quickly they shot an arrow in his back, which caused him returne and barricado up the doores, whereupon the Salvages set fire on the house. Harisons Boy finding his Masters peece loaded, discharged it at randome, at which bare report the Salvages all fled . . .

Captain Ralph Hamor, a fighter like his brother, beat off an Indian attack "onely with spades, axes, and brickbats"; not all were so lucky. Not far from Martin's Hundred seventy-three were slain; a family living in a small house nearby did not learn of the tragedy until two days later. How many actually were murdered that bloody Good Friday is difficult to calculate, but the toll must have been about four hundred. Six members of the Council died. Yet the tragedy could have been far more horrible except for "one converted Infidell," an Indian, Chanco, who had spent the night with the Pace family. The savage's brother urged him to kill Pace, but the Indian refused. Pace had "used him as his sonne"; and "thousands of ours were by the meanes of this alone thus preserved." Before daybreak Pace, warned of the massacre, rowed to Jamestown. An alarm was spread to the surrounding plantations.

When the numbness and shock of the massacre wore off, the colonists tried to find some good in the bloody business. Now they would be justified in destroying all the Indians by any method possible. If before there had been any deep sense of hesitancy in driving the Indians from their own lands that restraint could be comfortably dismissed. Again, a more practical view had to be taken toward the Indians; the easier course was "to civilize them by conquest than faire means." The bitter lesson must never be forgotten—to treat these savages as friends, to give them welcome in the houses of the settlers and access to the weapons of the colony, invited other treacheries. Religion was part of the spirit of the age, and to Christianize the heathen had appealed to English pride and duty; but between morning and nightfall on Good Friday in 1622 a revolution was wrought in the minds of early Virginians.

Among the survivors of the massacre was a gentle, modest, pious man, who had reached Jamestown in 1619. Little is known about the youth of George Sandys. The records show that in December, 1559 he entered St. Mary Hall, Oxford, but apparently took no degree; seven years later he was admitted to Middle Temple. His first published work, appearing in 1615, was a popular and authoritative account of a tour to France, Turkey, Italy, Egypt and Palestine.

Transplanted to Virginia, nothing in the activities of George Sandys suggested the bookish scholar. He commanded a punitive force against the Tappahannock Indians and offered to lead an expedition in search of a route to the Great South Sea. His commercial interests included building the first watermill in America, sponsoring the manufacture of iron, engaging in glassmaking and saying of the workmen sent him "a more damned crew hell never vomited," and endeavoring to revive silk and grape culture. The introduction of shipbuilding in the colony also is credited to this man, who served the colony as treasurer, was three times appointed a member of the council, and managed a plantation of fifteen hundred acres.

In London bookstalls in 1626, appeared a volume entitled *Ovid's Metamorphosis Englished by George Sandys.* The book of verses, dedicated to Charles I, admitted that these lines of poetry were "limned by that imperfect light which was snatched from the hours of night and repose." How clearly the picture emerges—the dark night, the flickering candle, the firelight, the scratching quill, the quiet and sensitive eyes of the first man in America to devote himself to literature and scholarship. A remembered sentence in John Smith's *Description of Virginia* seems suddenly to capture a setting wherein the mind of a poet could unfold: "The country is not mountanous nor yet low but such pleasant plaine hils and fertile valleyes, one prettily crossing an other, and watered so conveniently with their sweete brookes and christall springs, as if art it selfe had devised them."

Before leaving England George Sandys had translated

five books of the *Metamorphosis;* now in Virginia, building his watermill and ships, making his iron and glass, his mind sang the stanzas of Ovid's last ten books. The magnitude of his gift as a poet could not be denied. Pope declared stoutly that "English poetry owes much of its present beauty" to Sandy's translations. With the appearance in 1632 of a second complete handsome edition of the Ovid, Sandys included also Book I of Virgil's *Aeneid.* The literary stature of the man continued to grow with other works that included poetic paraphrases of the Psalms of David, the hymns of the Old and New Testament, and the Song of Solomon. "What you desire is not mortal," once philosophized Ovid, the unhappy exile on the shores of the Black Sea; and along the James, in a New World and a self-imposed exile, Sandys heard the echo of his voice across the centuries.

A census of Virginia, taken during the winter of 1624-25, counted one hundred and twenty-four persons in Jamestown, including adults, children, servants and Negroes; there were twenty-two houses, three stores, and a church; there were one-hundred and eighty-one cattle, one horse, two hundred and nine swine, and one hundred and twenty-one goats; against the threat of future attack, the town could count four pieces of mounted ordnance, ninety-two small arms, sixty swords, seventy-nine coats of mail, twenty pounds of powder, and one hundred and eighty pounds of shot. In August of 1624 James I won an old feud by dissolving the Virginia Company of London and making the colony part of his own royal government.

Within the limits of a one-crop agrarian community—and tobacco could be a jealous mistress, wearing out fertile fields and forcing farmers up the rivers and creeks in search of new acreage and easy transportation—Virginia prospered. The manner and style of the English gentry took root in this wilderness, producing independence of spirit and consciousness of social responsibility. If there were fewer of cavaliers than the romanticists would like to believe, so were there fewer spawn of Newgate Prison than the cynics sometimes suggest. In the years from 1635 to 1680 the influx of indentured servants may have averaged as high as sixteen hundred a year and likely not fewer than a thousand. In time these once landless people would push into the upper counties of the Tidewater, carrying with them the attitudes of the man who tilled the soil and felt a strength of mind as well as of body from that enterprise.

Out of this experience came the most significant characteristic of the Virginian, his disposition to manage his own affairs—a disposition that became a habit. Sir John Harvey, the royal governor in 1635, tried to impose an oppressive and tyrannical administration and found in the leadership of such Virginians as Captain Samuel

Mathews a spirited opposition. Above Newport News Mathews established a manor that by 1649 would employ its own weavers and shoemakers, support forty Negro servants that he would bring up "to trades in his house," grow its own wheat and barley, and raise an "abundance of kine, a brave dairy, swine great store, and poultry." As one who "keeps a good house, lives bravely, and [is] a true lover of Virginia" Mathews was deemed "worthy of much honour." Among the complaints against Harvey was that he detained "Letters to his Majestie the Lords and others concerning a contract," wrote Mathews, and "in open court" reviled "all the Councell," telling them "they were to give their attendance as assistants onely to advise with him." Harvey was truculent and arrogant, but Mathews and his followers stood on their rights and Mathews described a spirited scene:

> The next meeting [of the Council] in a most sterne manner he [Harvey] demanded the reason that wee had conceived of the countreye's Petition against him. Mr. Menefee made answer, the chiefest cause was the detayning of Letters to his Majestie and the Lords. Then he rising in a great rage sayd to Mr. Menefee; and do you say soe? He replied, yes: presently the governor in a fury went and striking him on the shoulder as hard as I can imagine he could said, I arrest you of suspicion of Treason to his Majestie. Then Captain Utie being neare said, and wee the like to you sir. Whereupon I seeing him in a rage,

> tooke him in my armes and said: Sir, there is no harm intended against you save only to acquaint you with the grievances of the Inhabitants and to the end I desire you to sitt downe in youre chayre . . .

Later the Council arrested Harvey and shipped him to England. In a huff the king sent his royal governor back, but the Virginia Council persevered and brought Harvey to trial. The Privy Council in England appointed another governor. As Englishmen, the Virginians had insisted on their rights and won them by due process of law. The triumph was considerable.

After Harvey, the story of Jamestown for modern Americans makes a long leap to 1676, when Virginia was torn by a strange little civil war called Bacon's Rebellion. Generally the intervening Cromwellian wars in the Mother Country provided a period when colonial America minded its own affairs and grew more deeply into its own habits and attitudes. Cromwell did little to enforce the unpopular Navigation Acts of 1651 and Virginia lived comfortably under three Roundhead governors. With the ascension of Charles II to the throne a more active interest was taken in the colonies and a second navigation act turned the alert Dutch to cultivating their own tobacco in the East Indies and tended to release inflationary pressure in Virginia by lowering the price of tobacco while raising the cost of imports from England. Quickly, the whole colony seemed to become unstrung, and three sets of human factors determined the subsequent disruption. One was the personality of Sir William Berkeley; another was the personality of Nathaniel Bacon, Jr.; and a third was the now distinct personality of the Englishman in Virginia.

Berkeley served two terms as governor, and his first term, beginning in 1642 and continuing about ten years, found him a reasonable and popular administrator. Sir William was filled with zeal and ambition, and was fiercely uncompromising in his loyalty to the Crown and the State Church, qualities that were virtues in a royal governor. During the years when Virginia was administered by three Roundhead governors, Sir William kept to his orchards at Green Spring, where he had planted some two thousand apple, pear, quince, peach and apricot trees. Were these, as some believe, years of brooding that left traces of excessive irritability and narrow irascibility upon the character of Sir William? Perhaps so; but this image of the old Royalist, biding his time in petulant reverie, is a tool for romanticists who wish to see in the events of his later years the first flowering of democracy.

Actually something quite different appears to have occurred. By now the best lands had come almost entirely into the hands of the upper or ruling class. For many indentured servants, gaining their freedom, the future was not altogether sunny. The competition with the slave already had become a real factor with which the poor white must contend; and, logically, his general choice was to push instead deeper into the wilderness, clearing his own land, possibly buying a slave or two but probably depending more on the help of his wife and children in beating back the forests. The romantic view would see in these circumstances a foreshadowing of those impulses that in time produced the great humanistic revolution whereby all men were declared as created equal; but another view is likewise valid and can argue that what was being seeded in Virginia grew into the tap roots of the War Between the States.

When King Charles II came to the throne in 1660, he was pleased to tender a new commission to Berkeley, and Virginians were not especially overwrought by that decision. Succeeding years produced a changing emotional and political climate, but again the causes can be romanticized to distorted perspectives. The Virginia spirit of managing its own internal affairs had existed before the reign of the easygoing Roundhead governors; the spirit now simply covered more ground, included new groups. Falling tobacco prices and the imposition of a steep poll tax worked directly, and with natural emotion, upon that spirit within the struggling frontiersman. Indian raids along the frontier heightened the tensions. A man, in these circumstances, would have been something more than a fool if he had not asked, rather sullenly, why Berkeley did not take punitive action against these marauders? And a man, sick at falling tobacco prices, strapped by the poll tax, would have been something more than a fool's fool if he hadn't grumbled that Berkeley must be up to some tricky purpose in permitting the House of Burgesses to sit like the Long Parliament. Sir William displayed no genius for comprehending the impending crisis, nor did he lift a hand to prevent it. The cruel joke in Jamestown that asked if Sir William had addressed anyone as a rogue or a dog, because if he hadn't he must be in one of his good moods doubtless exaggerated the facts; yet Sir William had become an object of ridicule, and in politics ridicule is invariably the mask of resentment and distrust.

Looking back on the rebellion that followed in 1676, one wishes that the causes were not so obscure. The records that exist obviously were written both to conceal and to reveal the truth. If one must see the revolt as an uprising of the oppressed frontiersman, then one has to explain what William Byrd I was doing lending early support to the conflict and dropping the whole affair like a hot potato when reforms were mentioned. The central figure in the rebellion, Nathaniel Bacon, Jr., was no yeoman of the guard. Bacon was the only son of a wealthy English squire. Educated at Cambridge and Gray's Inn, he was twenty-six when he reached Virginia. A tall man, some say that he had a swarthy complexion, others that he possessed a melancholy eye.

Berkeley accepted Bacon for what he was, an aristocrat, and appointed him to the Council, revealing some element of flexibility in this stout old Anglican since there were whispers that Bacon "tended to atheism." Yet Bacon established a fine plantation at Curles Neck on the James and a second estate on the site of "Bacon's Quarter Branch" near Richmond, and it would have been difficult, in that age, to concede that so much wealth could stem from any large amount of godlessness. Other traits in Bacon emerged, as Virginians came to know him. A hot head, impatient, prone to excitability—in such phrases the tall figure of the fellow assumes an angry erectness and the melancholy eye begins to glitter.

To justify his armed revolt against the governor Bacon issued "The Declaration of the People." What the document reveals as much as anything—perhaps all it reveals —is a list of abuses that even landed, influential Englishmen found unendurable. Bacon charged Berkeley with using "specious pretences of Publick works" to raise "unjust Taxes" and advance "private Favourits and other sinnister ends." Again, Bacon declared that during Berkeley's long administration the governor had not "in any measure advanced this hopefull Colony either by Fortifications, Townes or Trade." Again Sir William had pushed into "places of judicature scandalous and Ignorant favourits" and had assumed "the monopoley of the Beaver Trade." Again he had "protected favoured and Imboldened the Indians" without providing "proper meanes of satisfaction for their many Invasion Murthers and Robberies Committed upon us."

Add to such grievances falling tobacco prices, high poll taxes, a House of Burgesses that had set like the Long Parliament, and the Rebellion becomes understandable. One of our brilliant scholars of colonial America, Louis B. Wright, catches the war in proper perspective:

> To interpret Bacon's Rebellion as a forecast of the American Revolution or as clear proof of the development of the American system of democracy on the frontier, is hardly accurate, but this conflict was an omen of things to come. It was an indication of the spirit of independence engendered among settlers in a region where the acquisition of landed freeholds was easy; it was a declaration that the whole body of freemen would demand the rights which Englishmen were guaranteed under the common law; and it was a warning that the aristocratic system imitative of the English country gentry would have to be adaptable and on guard against political corruption if it hoped to survive.*

Bacon's Rebellion traces its source to the summer of 1675 when a band of Susquehannas, driven south by the

* Louis B. Wright, *The Atlantic Frontier* (New York, 1947) p. 83.

Senecas, crossed into Virginia and stole a number of swine. An expedition of settlers under Colonel George Mason and Major George Brent pursued these vandals, and, rather losing their heads, killed some Susquehannas (among them a chief) who had been innocent of any misdemeanor. Bloody Indian reprisals followed. Next a larger force of Maryland and Virginia settlers under Colonel John Washington descended on an Indian town, where five chiefs came out for a parley. Apparently the chiefs were slain and apparently no one quite knew why. For seven weeks siege was laid to the town, then with an unexpected show of force one night the Indians escaped.

Indian raids quickened during January of 1676, and the toll of dead rose in settlements at the heads of Virginia's rivers. Frontier forts, for all they cost a pretty penny to maintain, were so widely separated that they offered scant protection. Berkeley's refusal to send the militia to punish the Indians rankled an incensed people, who suspected the governor wished to make no move that would upset his own profitable trading with the Indians. "No bullets could pierce beaver skins," they said, echoing Bacon. In the upper counties settlers banded into a force of about three hundred volunteers, and persuaded Bacon, already angered by the murder of an overseer, to take command of this little army.

Bacon requested Berkeley to grant him a commission as leader of the volunteers, but the governor evaded the issue. Meanwhile Bacon had to find subsistence for his soldiers, and when the supposedly friendly Occaneechee Indians kept stalling in supplying this need—another evasion that many believed the governor inspired—Bacon wearied of the delay and a number of Occaneechees were killed. Berkeley declared Bacon in rebellion, ordered his force disbanded, and set out with a small force of his own to intercept Bacon and his rebels. The two groups, happily, failed to collide; and Berkeley, returning to Jamestown, should hardly have been flattered by the tenor of public sentiment. In a burst of prudence, the governor ordered a new election of burgesses. Never has a well-laid plan of mice and men gone more astray. Henrico County elected Bacon to the House, the last thing Berkeley wanted. The governor's series of moves now included a decision first to arrest Bacon and then to keep him out of the Assembly by restoring him to the Council. In the midst of these crafty maneuvers the Assembly, taking matters into its own hands, declared war on the Indians, named young Bacon commander of its forces, and left the governor little choice but to acquiesce in that decision.

The next steps in the affair seem like comic opera. Bacon waited several days for Berkeley to send his commission. Nothing happened. Either because his wife was ill or he distrusted the governor's double dealing (and very possibly for both reasons) Bacon returned to his home at Curles Neck. A week later Bacon came back to

Jamestown, formed his troops on the green "not a flight shot distant" from the state house, summoned the burgesses by drum beat, and proceeded with a guard to the state house. Near a corner of the building he encountered Berkeley. The subsequent scene finds its first high moment in the governor reputedly baring his chest and inviting Bacon to shoot him. Bacon's reply was that he wanted a commission to shoot Indians. Some say that at this point one of Bacon's guards levelled his gun at the burgesses in the window, demanding the commission. Some say that Bacon cried, "Dam my blood, I'll kill governor and Council, Assembly and all, and then I'll sheathe my sword in my own heart's blood." Some say that one of the burgesses, keeping his wits, avoided this possible slaughter by waving "a pacifick hankercher" and promising the commission. Next day on the second attempt the Assembly proffered a commission that Bacon found acceptable and granted him also a pardon from all previous acts.

In brighter spirits Bacon set off for the falls of the James to fight Indians. Berkeley went to Gloucester, raised his own force of militia and again declared Bacon in rebellion. Public sentiment, even among the militia, strongly favored Bacon, who now turned back toward Gloucester, and Berkeley, in another burst of prudence, crossed the Chesapeake to Accomac. Bacon then established his headquarters at Middle Plantation (later renamed Williamsburg) and proclaimed as traitors Berkeley and his Council. He called a meeting of the Assembly for September fourth and sent an armed vessel to capture Berkeley at Accomac. The evidence is that this mission failed through "indescretion and the juice of the grape," doubtless inspiring Bacon to an early attempt at prohibition by revoking the licenses of all inns, alehouses and tippling-houses, except those at Jamestown and at the two ferries of the York River, where the sale of beer and cider was permitted. Again Bacon sallied forth to fight the Indians, joined another force of about four hundred volunteers sent to capture him, and drove the Indians from their refuge in the marshes of the York River. Meanwhile Berkeley, raising an army of six hundred men, sailed from Accomac to Jamestown. Bacon marched to combat "with his Small tired Body of men . . . and advancing on horseback himselfe on the Sandy Beech before the Towne commands the Trumpet to sound, Fires his carbyne, dismounts, surveys the Ground and orders a French worke [i.e., a trench] to be cast up."

Through the night the defenses were built "by the help of the moone light . . . although they had but two axes and 2 spades." At daybreak "six of Bacons Soldiers ran up to the Pallasadees of the Towne and Fired briskly upon the Guard, retreating Safely without any damage." Berkeley commanded, reportedly, that no gun should be fired "upon paine of death, pretending to be loath to spill bloode and much more to be Beginner of it." Bacon now, "having planted his great Guns," seized "the wives and female Relations of such Gentlemen as were in the Governor's Service against him" and placed them "in the Face of his Enemy, as Bulworkes for their Battery." Understandably the governor "was at last over persuaded, nay hurryed away against his owne Will to Accomack and forced to leave the Towne to the mercy of the enemy." Next morning Bacon entered Jamestown, and "soldier like considering of what importance a Place of that Refuge was, . . . instantly resolves to lay it level with the ground, and the same night he became possessed of it, sett Fire to Towne, church and state house (wherein were the Countryes Records which Drummond had privately convey'd thence and preserved from Burning). The towne consisted of 12 new brick Houses besides a considerable number of Frame houses with brick chimneys, all of which will not be rebuilt (as is computed) for Fifteen hundred pounds of Tobacco."

Bacon took over Berkeley's home at Green Spring and planned new reforms. Then, journeying into Gloucester county, he came down with fever. Upon his death he was buried secretly and a poem of the day extolled:

> Here let him rest, while we this truth report,
> He's gone from hence unto a higher court
> To plead his cause, where he by this doth know
> Whether to Caesar he was friend or foe.

Restored to power, Berkeley hanged twenty-three of those who had supported Bacon's Rebellion. Finally, after twice being summoned home by the king, he left Virginia in May, 1677.

In 1685 the State House was rebuilt at Jamestown, but in 1698 a fire destroyed the structure and the decision was reached the following year to move the capital to Middle Plantation or Williamsburg—"a healthier and more convenient Place," said an early 18th century source, "and freer from the Annoyance of *Muskettoes.*" The main building of the College of William and Mary (founded in 1693), several houses, a tavern or ordinary, a few stores, a brick church, and a graveyard were the whole of Williamsburg then, but quickly the town grew into a proud and prosperous community. Meanwhile at Jamestown the original settlement was soon described as "nothing but Abundance of Brick Rubbish, and three or four good inhabited Houses, tho' the Parish is of pretty large Extent, but less than others." A new century began, and developed a character of its own. But many decades intervened before the forces inherent within the new age produced changes that shook the world.

WILLIAMSBURG

Cradle of Revolution

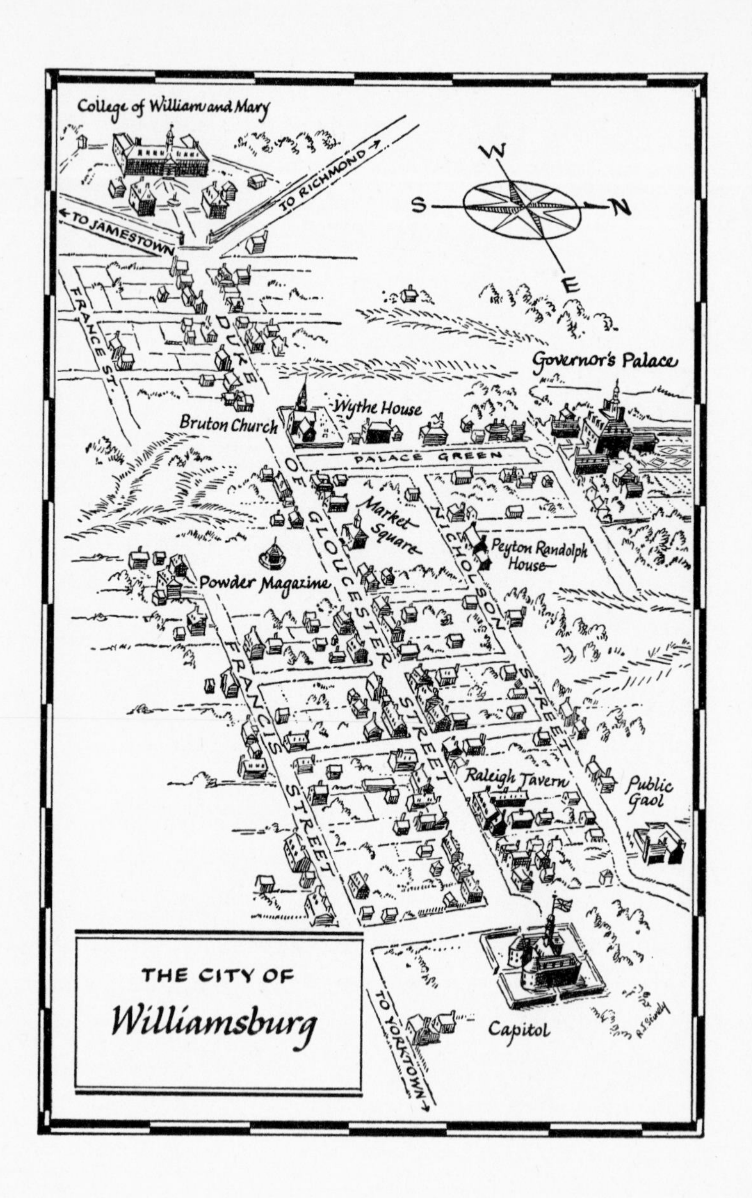

College of William and Mary
TO RICHMOND
TO JAMESTOWN
W
S
N
E
FRANCE ST.
DUKE
Governor's Palace
Wythe House
Bruton Church
PALACE GREEN
OF GLOUCESTER STREET
Market Square
NICHOLSON STREET
Peyton Randolph House
Powder Magazine
FRANCIS STREET
Raleigh Tavern
Public Gaol
THE CITY OF
Williamsburg
TO YORKTOWN
Capitol

4

Decade of Criſis

THESE Virginians who moved their capital from Jameſtown to Williamsburg in 1699 remained Englishmen in heart and mind, and the fashion of calling themselves "British Americans" was a vogue of much later date. For the next three-quarters of a century anyone who walked along Duke of Glouceſter Street, dined at Raleigh Tavern, ſtrolled the gardens of the Palace, or visited in the homes of the city recognized immediately that Williamsburg was a planters' capital. John Rolfe's weed, once so scorned by James I, had built many fine plantations by now—some in the Piedmont beyond the fall line of Virginia's rivers, but more in that fertile coaſtal region known as the Tidewater. The proprietors and heirs of those plantations, visiting Williamsburg on pleasure and business, reflected the "manners" of the southern colonies that Edmund Burke included among the "six capital sources" of the freedom-loving American character.

For more than seventy years after 1699 the relationship

between the royal governors of Virginia and their subjects was generally cordial, and in many instances even affectionate. The gracious plan that gave Williamsburg its wide Duke of Gloucester Street, the green at Market Square, the approach to the Palace between borders of catalpa trees, revealed in Francis Nicholson (governor, 1698-1705) an understanding of, and a respect for, the essential qualities of these Englishmen of Virginia. Pride in position, class, appearance—what traits could be more fundamentally British? The houses of Williamsburg, the dress of the Virginia gentleman and his lady reflected more than English influence; they were symbols of the English tradition successfully transplanted three thousand miles from the homeland. What could be more British than the love of gardens? Or of furniture created by the genius of a Chippendale or Hepplewhite?

The "Publick Times" in Williamsburg—when the House of Burgesses, the Council or the courts convened—were again evidence, as Burke declared, that the colonists were "not only devoted to liberty, but liberty according to English ideas, and on English principles." In no small measure, when in 1765 the Stamp Act began a decade of crisis, the crux of the revolt that followed resided in an astonishing fact. The great representative men in Williamsburg like Washington and Jefferson, Wythe and Bland, Patrick Henry and George Mason clung more tenaciously to British traditions than did the king and his ministers across the ocean. To read Jefferson's Declaration of Independence, grievance by grievance, is to realize how completely in Virginian eyes George III and Lords North, Townshend and Grenville had lost touch with the main current of their own intellectual history. Burke would speak of "a nation which I hope still respects, and formerly adored, liberty," coming to the nub of a crisis with a perception that was not, unfortunately, practical English politics.

In later years John Adams remarked that "The Revolution was effected before the war commenced. The Revolution was in the minds and hearts of the people." Again Adams commented: "This radical change in the principles, opinions, sentiments, and affections of the people, was the real American Revolution." The story of Williamsburg in the decade of crisis beginning in 1765—the story that gives Williamsburg profound and continuing significance to the modern visitor—finds its great men spelling out in actions clear definitions of those "principles, opinions, sentiments, and affections." Yet what tenets could be more deeply rooted in the English character than a respect for representative government, a belief in the supremacy of law, a dedication to constitutionalism, and a devotion to the liberty of the individual? One by one these became the issues at stake through the heart-wrenching decade; one by one, at its ominous conclusion, they would be the violated principles producing the Declaration of Independence.

Vainly Burke endeavored to make a headstrong king, a fickle Parliament, a shortsighted Cabinet realize wherein they were forcing a rebellion: "An Englishman is the unfittest person on earth to argue another Englishman into slavery." The causes were many and complicated, the core of the crisis undeniable. On one side of the ocean, George III, North, Townshend, Grenville, considered themselves so well schooled in statecraft that they would rule by quick-tempered expediencies even though they must turn back the clock of English history to do so; and on the other, men like Bland and Peyton Randolph and Wythe, Washington, Patrick Henry and Jefferson, made the science of government one wherein natural rights once won must never be surrendered.

The Englishmen of Virginia were driven to revolt; the break was made with difficulty, for they found in their hearts that it was a hard and grudging decision to make. Yet these were men who moved on the stream of their age. Dr. Whitfield J. Bell, Jr. is perceptive in describing the eighteenth century as "the last age of the brilliant amateurs" when "an English dissenting clergyman, Joseph Priestley, discovered a new chemical element, oxygen; a German bandmaster, William Herschel, found a new planet, Uranus; and a Philadelphia printer, Franklin, established the science of electricity."* If in Williamsburg, one of the vital centers of a rising nation, other great amateurs groped for a form of government that might maintain justice and yield to all a right to "life, liberty and the pursuit of happiness," the age and the men must be seen as reasonable partners.

The Stamp Act became a law on March 22, 1765, effective November 1 following, but this intelligence had not reached Williamsburg when in early May members of the House of Burgesses pushed doggedly toward the conclusion of their labors. The previous October, and again in December when the House had met as a Committee of the Whole, the proposed stamp taxes had been roundly denounced. At the forefront of the opposition had stood Richard Henry Lee, ardent student of history, expert in Roman and English law, heir to one of Virginia's biggest fortunes, and inclined upon occasion to pursue causes and courses that gave his more conservative friends moments of discomfiture.

First elected to the House from Westmoreland County in 1761, Lee's excessive diffidence had made many wonder if he would ever take part in their debates; then, on a motion "to lay so heavy a duty on the importation of

* Whitfield J. Bell Jr., "The Father of All Yankees: Benjamin Franklin" in *The American Story,* edited by Earl Schenck Miers (New York, 1956), p. 71.

slaves as effectually to put an end to the iniquitous and disgraceful traffic within the colony of Virginia," passion loosened Lee's tongue. Thereafter no one questioned either Lee's power as an orator or the bold, penetrating mind behind his high forehead; and for generations abolitionists seized joyfully upon his arguments. The Stamp Act again found Lee anything but shy; he not only moved that a committee be appointed to send to the Mother Country representations against the proposed measure, but two of the three documents that evolved from this committee were his compositions. True, the more cautious minds on the committee and notably George Wythe, Virginia's most distinguished jurist, tried to dull the edge of Lee's writings. Gentle as only the natural teacher can be, molder in no small measure of the remarkable minds that belonged to Jefferson and John Marshall and Henry Clay, a man who every morning danced himself awake under a shower of cold well water, Wythe's talents rarely appeared limited. In the case of Lee's "Memorial" to the House of Lords, however, the deftness and the softness of the Wythe touch did not go far enough, at least for Governor Francis Fauquier who found "very warm and indecent" the declaration that Virginians

> . . . conceive it to be a fundamental Principle of the *British* Constitution, without which Freedom can no

> Where exist, that the People are not subject to any Taxes but such as are laid on them by their own Consent, or by those who are legally appointed to represent them: Property must become too precarious for the Genius of a free People which can be taken from them at the Will of others, who cannot know what Taxes such People can bear, or the easiest Mode of raising them; and who are not under that Restraint, which is the greatest Security against a burthensome Taxation, when the Representatives themselves must be affected by every Tax imposed on the People.

In view of the high-spirited opposition the proposal of these taxes had elicited, there is magnificent humor in the governor's comment that toward mid-May there "crept into the House" a copy of the Stamp Act. If Fauquier anticipated another hostile eruption, he was, at least momentarily, pleasantly disappointed. The burgesses reacted with a helpless discouragement amounting to inertia. Their attitude said, in effect, that a bad law had been passed and the devil take it. Hot, muggy weather loomed, and the empty benches in the House indicated that a number of members already had started the long, tedious journeys home.

And there the story might have ended except that one drowsy afternoon a rather thin-boned fellow with his hair worn in a greased pigtail rode down Duke of Gloucester Street on a lean horse. His name was Patrick Henry and he was the new member of the House from Louisa County. Those who pried into his background found many of the facts anything but romantic: he had failed as a storekeeper; he had failed as a farmer; and with not much choice left had studied law for six weeks and received a license—more for his promise than his accomplishments as a student. Yet, diligent and energetic, he had managed almost twelve hundred cases in the next three years. He was a talker in a rough, easygoing, God-given way; as one critic observed, "He sounded the recesses and depths of the human heart." Among the individualistic, strongly opinionated Presbyterians, Baptists and Quakers whom he served, the fellow fitted like a pea in a pod.

Virginia had taken its first notice of Patrick Henry in the "Parson's Cause" in 1763. The case had been brought by the Reverend James Maury, a minister of the established church, who sued to recover his salary, fixed at sixteen thousand pounds of tobacco. When a short crop greatly advanced the market value of tobacco, an act of the Assembly had commuted the salaries of ministers into money at the rate of two pence per pound, the former price of tobacco. The king did not approve the act, but the burgesses decided to enforce it. In defending the law (and by so doing, challenging the authority of the Crown to disallow colonial statutes), Henry used all his gifts of oratory, and not a few of his tricks—in the controlled rise and fall of his voice, in the long fingers that he waved or clasped or held at a thoughtful point to emphasize an argument. As sometimes happened, words ran away with him and there were reputed murmurs of treason when he contended that "a king, by disallowing acts of a salutary nature, from being the father of his people, degenerates into a tyrant, and forfeits all rights to his subjects' obedience." Afterward Henry confessed to poor Maury that he had only taken the case "to render himself popular." One hopes that he kept a straight face. At one point in his arguments he had characterized members of the clergy as "rapacious harpies."

Firebrand, opportunist, "a son of thunder"—with varying degrees of justice these epithets applied to the Patrick Henry who on May 23, 1765 rose in the House to make his first speech as the new member from Louisa County. John Robinson, who had served the colony for better than a quarter of a century as both speaker of the House and treasurer, had proposed a plan for relieving the money shortage in the colony by setting up a public loan office. If Robinson's talents were limited, his personal charm and family connections made him a bulwark of the Old Guard. Henry nonetheless was vigorous in his attack on Robinson's plan; he had come to Williamsburg to make his voice heard and his presence known as spokesman for the up country. Robinson naturally commanded the support to push his measure through the House, though the Council killed it.

Meanwhile behind the scenes in Williamsburg one of the busiest men was John Fleming, a political power in the same up country that had sired Henry. The conservative Tidewater crowd who believed nothing further could or should be done about the Stamp Act, now that it was law, found short sympathy with Fleming. Perhaps Fleming, perhaps Henry, drew up the seven resolutions against these "usurpations of parliament" that were in Henry's pocket when on the twenty-ninth he again took the floor. Five of the resolutions were offered, but the conservatives gained a chance to gather their wits by putting off until next day consideration of the measures.

Still, the time was brief for the opposition to marshal forces, and the earlier departure for home of many Tidewater members now seemed almost like the baiting of a trap. Among those who rallied in the common cause with George Wythe and Speaker Robinson was Richard Bland. On all questions touching the rights and privileges of the colony, Bland was the authority; there was no phase of the colony's settlement and progress that he did not know. In the more than twenty years that this gifted classical scholar had served in the House his gentleness, his affability, his quiet manner, his thoughtfulness had become respected traits. In December Bland had written one of the three protests to the Mother Country against the proposed stamp taxes, and, in character, had traced the historical rights of the colonists to be treated as "Britons." Yet it was no contradiction that he now opposed the resolutions of Henry and Fleming, or that in another year in *An Inquiry into the Rights of British Colonies* he would reveal a bold mind that grasped clearly and fully the emerging crisis. It was "not on any Difference of Opinion," wrote Jefferson, that men like Bland opposed the resolutions, "but because those Papers of the preceding Session had already expressed the same Sentiments and Assertions of Right, and that an Answer to them was yet to be expected." The compulsive intemperance of Fleming and Henry, their refusal to let government proceed in an orderly fashion, their stubborn shortsightedness in not recognizing that even defiance must have its time and place constituted dangerous heresies to the conservative mind and temperament.

A similar distrust became natural to Peyton Randolph, who had been a force in the affairs of Virginia since his appointment as king's attorney general in 1748. The stature and quality of this man had emerged in the pistole fee controversy. The value of a pistole is variously estimated, but the coin was worth about four dollars; and the demand by Governor Robert Dinwiddie that this fee be paid for the use of the public seal on all land patents impressed the burgesses as an unjust tax. Socially Dinwiddie and Randolph were warm friends, but each now, by his own view, stood on a principle. So in 1754 Randolph went to London to plead the unconstitutionality of the pistole fee, and Dinwiddie, angered that Randolph had gone abroad without consent on a hostile mission, suspended the absent attorney. Appointed in his place, Wythe accepted the post with tongue in cheek, intending to hold the office only until his friend returned. Next the conflict between the governor and the burgesses turned to a bitter struggle over the fee of twenty-five hundred pounds that Randolph had been promised for his mission to London; when the sum was tacked as a rider to a bill for twenty thousand pounds to carry on the Indian War, an exasperated governor dismissed the Assembly. Meanwhile in London the Lords of Trade ordered the pistole fee reduced and requested Randolph's reinstatement. For both Randolph and the governor the situation had become embarrassing; Dinwiddie asserted, "I am not inflexible," and Randolph, admitting that his activities had been somewhat irregular, was restored to office. Loyalty and respect for authority, the fundamental requisite for any orderly process of government, also had been restored, not as a principle but in degree of emphasis. Dinwiddie's huffiness stemmed more from personal feeling than legal affront. Where else should Englishmen turn for the redress of grievance if not to the Mother Country?

Unless logic and fair play in colonial affairs could be thus maintained, then for a Randolph, a Bland, a Wythe the earth shook and the old world crumbled. So, in the decade now beginning, would events move for Peyton Randolph, intensely opposed to the precipitate resolutions of Henry and Fleming in 1765, and nine years later becoming president of the First Continental Congress. So, too, would events move for the gifted Edmund Pendleton, who already had practiced law for twenty years and had served in the House for thirteen; eleven years hence he would preside over the convention that adopted his resolution instructing the Virginia delegates to the Continental Congress to propose independence from Britain.

No mere struggle between the Tidewater and the Piedmont for political power could explain the drama that began the fateful decade in Williamsburg. Too much of heart and mind and spiritual faith were involved. Peyton Randolph, with his brother John, had been two of the examiners when Patrick Henry had applied for his license, and we have the word of Jefferson that although the Randolphs realized Henry was "very ignorant of the law," they recognized that he was "a man of genius." Yet to any Williamsburg conservative Henry's was a new kind of genius, born of environmental influences and values that were rough-hewn, tough-fibered, stubbornly independent, and it produced a type of personality that would always rub against conservative temperaments with a sort of flinty irritation. It was small wonder, then, that on first contact the sparks flew.

On May thirtieth, when the five resolutions were brought to a vote, the victory clearly belonged to Patrick Henry. In the first resolution Henry contended that the original settlers had "brought with them, and transmitted to their Posterity, and all other" the "Privileges, Franchises, and Immunities, that have at any Time been held, enjoyed, and possessed by the People of Great Britain." The second resolution declared that the two royal charters granted by James I entitled the colonists to the privileges, liberties and immunities "as if they had been abiding and born within the Realm of England"; the third that only the people or their representatives can know "what Taxes the People are able to bear, and the easiest Mode of raising them" and that if this "distinguishing Characteristick of British Freedom" is denied "the ancient Constitution cannot subsist"; while the fourth stressed the fact that the king and British people must acknowledge Virginians "have uninteruptedly enjoyed the Right of being thus governed by their own Assembly, in the Article of their Taxes and Internal Police." The fifth resolution, the center of the gathering storm, declared:

> Therefore that the General Assembly of this Colony have the sole Right & Power to lay Taxes &

> Impositions upon the Inhabitants of this Colony and that every Attempt to vest such Power in any Person or Persons whatsoever other than the General Assembly aforesaid has a manifest Tendency to destroy British as well as American Freedom.

Doubtless there was much truth in Edmund Randolph's assertion that Henry "indulged in a strain never before heard in the Royal Capitol," yet in no sense was the emotionalism of the day one-sided. A "French Traveller" reached Williamsburg at noon that May thirtieth, and the sight of three Negroes hanging from the gallows for a theft of three hundred pounds did not match the excitement afforded at the Capitol.

The Frenchman attended the "very strong Debates" on the five resolutions, and reported: "Shortly after I Came in one of the members stood up and said he had read that in former times tarquin and Julus, had their Brutus, Charles had his Cromwell, and he Did not Doubt but some good american would stand up, in favour of his Country." Henry's angry outburst brought Robinson to his feet. That was treason, the speaker declared. He was sorry to see that, in the account of the French visitor, "not one of the members of the house was loyal Enough to stop him, before he had gone so far . . ." Tradition has long insisted that Henry flung back defiantly, "If this be treason, make the most of it!" But the French visitor recorded another version. Henry, the Frenchman said, asked the pardon of the speaker and the House if he had offended either. Moreover, "he would shew his loyalty to his majesty King G. the third, at the Expence of the last Drop of his blood . . ." Indeed, if he had uttered anything treasonable he had been misled by "the heat of passion"; again he begged the pardon of all concerned; whereupon "some other Members stood up and backed him on which that afaire was Droped."

Enough excitement remained, however, to keep the French visitor entertained. One by one the resolutions were put to a vote. Henry's best margin was 22 to 17, but on the fifth resolution strong hope persisted that Henry could be beaten. The scene in the old Capitol with crowds listening at the door, the windows opened to give the relief of fresh air to flushed cheeks and hot tempers, the burgesses squirming on their wooden benches and standing and whispering, glances darting across the room in shrewd appraisal of how far this one or that was now ready to follow Henry down the road of near-treason—in imagination it is not difficult to see that passionate moment when the tally was announced. The ayes, 20; the nays, 19!

Thomas Jefferson, scarcely a month past his twenty-second birthday, listened to the debates and in later years would "well remember" after the vote on the fifth resolution how Peyton Randolph "came out at the Door where

I was standing, and exclaimed, 'By God, I would have given one Hundred guineas for a single vote.'" Others believed Jefferson should have jogged his memory; Randolph had offered five hundred guineas for a vote that would have divided the House so that Robinson in the chair could "have negatived the Resolution."

Well satisfied, Henry left for home, yet the aroused conservatives were in no mood to concede defeat. Next morning young Jefferson watched Colonel Peter Randolph "thumbing over the Volumes of Journals to find a Precedent of expunging a Vote of the House," although Jefferson could not recall "whether he found the Erasure." The point became academic. To use Jefferson's phrase, "some of the more timid members," remembering their votes of the previous day, "had become alarmed" and were quite content with or without precedent to have the fifth resolution voted out of the record. The "French Traveller" also returned to the Capitol "and heard very hot Debates stil about the Stamp Dutys." But even with the fifth resolution expunged, the French visitor penned a sad ending: "Upon which the Governor Disolved the assembly, which hinderd their proceeding."

Quickly through the colonies spread intelligence of Henry's speeches and the five resolutions. In Rhode Island and Massachusetts newspapers garbled the story to the point where the resolutions declared that anyone who asserted the right of taxation did not rest exclusively with the General Assembly became "an enemy to his Majesty's colony." Yet the Bostonian who, on his deathbed, cried, "Oh! Those Virginians are men!" reflected the temper of the decade that had opened. Perhaps, as some said, Patrick Henry was the supreme opportunist. Sensitive to the popular spirit of his age, he never asked opportunity to knock twice.

The opposition to the passage of the Stamp Act, once released, grew rapidly into a militant force even in a Williamsburg that respected the conservative tradition. On November third Governor Fauquier wrote a letter to the Lords of Trade in London lamenting "the present unhappy State of this Colony." The governor's recital of the events that had occurred when Colonel Mercer arrived to take office as Distributor of Stamps contained this provocative passage:

> . . . The Crowd did not yet disperse, it was growing dark and I did not think it safe to leave Mr. *Mercer* behind me, so I again advanced to the Edge of the Steps, and said aloud I believed no Man there would do me any Hurt, and turned to Mr. *Mercer* & told him if he would walk with me through the People I believed I could conduct him safe to my House, and we accordingly walked Side by Side through the thickest of the People who did not molest us, tho' there was some little Murmurs. By my thus taking him under my Protection I believe I saved him from being insulted at least. . . .

After prudent reflection, Colonel Mercer resigned the office.

If Patrick Henry was among the first to ignite "the real American Revolution" that Adams insisted was effected in the hearts and minds of the people before the war began, the focus of the crisis quickly shifted to others.

In Williamsburg certainly none surpassed the reddish-haired young man who heard Peyton Randolph mutter he would have paid a small ransom for the single vote to squelch Henry. At seventeen Thomas Jefferson had come out of the rolling upland mountains to attend the College of William and Mary, and, if the legend can be trusted, applied himself to his studies fifteen or sixteen hours a day. Within two years he completed his course at the college and began to study law under George Wythe. A happy mating it proved, this union of two of the most remarkable minds in colonial America. "His virtue was of the purest kind, his integrity inflexible, his justice exact," wrote Jefferson in characterizing Wythe. "He might truly be called the Cato of his country, without the avarice of the Roman, for a more disinterested person never lived." Wythe, who taught one of his Negro slaves to read Latin and Greek, as both demanding tutor and warm-hearted friend opened a world of ever enlarging fascinations to Jefferson. He took young Jefferson to dine with Governor Fauquier, himself a man of unusual intellectual accomplishments; and often they were joined by Professor Small, scientist and most learned member of the College faculty. Wythe was the dominant influence in Williamsburg on Jefferson, the enduring teacher whom the student would describe as "the honor of his own and the model for future times."

Ideas passed so naturally between Wythe, the mentor, and Jefferson, the student, that it was not always possible to tell which belonged to the other. Yet Jefferson was strongly individualistic, a man of powerful inner resources who, upon his father's death, at the age of fifteen had taken over the management of the family plantation and had quickly demonstrated high administrative abilities. Through his lifetime he liked to call himself a farmer, and he possessed a strength of character that was like a fertile field with its ripening tobacco, a strength of naturalness, of elemental virtue. His affection for his parents, his sisters, and for Dabney Carr, his brother-in-law, revealed the emotional depth of Jefferson. It was right for him to carry a little violin with which he amused himself on the long journey between Charlottesville and Williamsburg, for music was in his heart, in his mind, and in the very meter of the prose he one day would write. He liked the excitement of horse races and was himself a fine horseman, but a single cock fight would so repel him that he would frame a law to abolish the barbarous sport. All of Jefferson's qualities Wythe seemed to understand, to develop; and the genius of Wythe, the teacher, was that Jefferson was left to become entirely the person that the Creator had intended him to be.

In 1766 the repeal of the Stamp Act brought a sense of relief to colonial America, and joyous New Yorkers voted to build statues of George III and William Pitt; then the Declaratory Act was passed, wherein Parliament proclaimed its power to bind the colonies "in all cases whatsoever," and the maturing mind behind Jefferson's hazel-gray eyes could not fail but sense the danger. Against the quickening crisis, the young man tried to build his own life. In 1767 he began the practice of law—the year when the Townshend Revenue Act imposed thoroughly unpopular duties on glass and lead, paint and tea. Jefferson married; Jefferson dreamed of building a spacious home upon his beloved mountaintop near Charlottesville; but in 1769 he was back in Williamsburg to take his seat in the House of Burgesses. Lord Botetourt, who had become governor upon the death of Fauquier, dissolved the Assembly for protesting against a proposal to transport prisoners to England for trial—a measure, asserted the burgesses, that deprived them of "the inestimable Privilege of being tried by a Jury from the Vicinage as well as the Liberty of summoning and producing Witnesses . . ." Such resolves, insisted the governor, "augur ill of their Effect"; yet not quite so ill as the resolution next day when the burgesses, assembling at Raleigh Tavern, pledged themselves not to buy British goods. The man who moved the adoption of this resolution was George Washington; the man who drafted it was his neighbor George Mason; and both, in the genesis of America as a nation, fulfilled the role of giants in the earth.

Washington called Williamsburg his "metropolis" and bore for the city the affection of a man who knew it intimately for more than three active, exciting decades. Here in a very real sense Washington came of age, for Williamsburg first saw him as a shy lad of seventeen who had made the long journey by horseback (from Mount Vernon) to obtain his surveyor's license at William and Mary College. He returned to accept a hazardous mission during the bitter winter of 1753-54 that took him a thousand miles from Williamsburg into western Pennsylvania to warn the French from encroaching on land that belonged to Britain. In 1756 Washington took his seat in the House of Burgesses; he did not relinquish it during the next sixteen years.

But Williamsburg as Washington's "metropolis" held much more personal associations. Here he brought his bride on his honeymoon; here he indulged his affection for the theatre and admired the same red-haired actress for four nights; here he worshipped in Bruton Parish Church and dined with such dearly loved friends as George Wythe and Peyton Randolph; here he danced at the Palace and roamed the shops for gifts for his step-children. There were townspeople in Williamsburg who, reading the published account of his journey into the Indian country, must have recognized as early as 1754 his gifts of courage, diplomacy and leadership. Surely Williamsburg must have repeated his comment at Fair Meadows: "I heard the bullets whistle, and, believe me, there is something charming in the sound"; someone had to repeat the remark, for it traveled across the seas and reached the ears of George II.

There were other moods to Washington that Williamsburg came to know. This big man who seemed to smother the reins in his large, strong hands when he rode a horse down Duke of Gloucester Street, was as Burke would have said "devoted . . . to liberty according to English ideas, and on English principles." As the decade of crisis ran on—in 1770 the Boston Massacre, in 1772 the affair off Providence, Rhode Island when New England patriots ran aground the armed British revenue schooner *Gaspée,* captured the crew and burned the vessel—Washington continued to emerge with a wholeness of character. In England the *Gaspée* affair might seem an act of piracy, but in Williamsburg the spirit of America's defiance to tyranny had been symbolized, and Washington contributed to the fireworks display that celebrated the event.

"For a considerable Time our Countrymen seemed to fall into a State of Insensibility to our Situation," Jefferson wrote in his *Autobiography*. The duty on tea and the threat of the Declaratory Act "still suspended over us," and the inquiry in Rhode Island following the *Gaspée* incident revived the danger that alleged crimes committed in America might be tried in England. Jefferson confessed to a device that demonstrated how deeply undercurrents had cut into Williamsburg since the closing days of May, 1765 when the resolutions on the Stamp Act had been debated:

> . . . Not thinking our old & leading Members up to the Point of Forwardness & Zeal which the Times required, Mr. *Henry, R. H. Lee,* Mr. *Francis L. Lee,* Mr. [Dabney] *Carr* & myself agreed to meet in the Evening in a private Room of the *Raleigh* to consult on the State of Things. There may have been a Member or two more whom I do not recollect. We were all sensible that the most urgent of all Measures was that of coming to an Understanding with all the other Colonies to consider the *British* Claims as a common Cause to all, & to produce an Unity of Action: and for this Purpose that a Comm[itt]ee of Correspond[en]ce in each Colony would be the best Instrument for Intercommunication: and that their first Measure would probably be to propose a Meeting of Deputies from every Colony at some central Place, who should be charged with the Direction of the Measures which should be taken by all. . . . It was so agreed . . . and a Commee of Correspondence appointed of whom *Peyton Randolph,* the Speaker, was Chairman. . . .

In addition to Chairman Randolph and those who had attended Jefferson's private meeting at Raleigh Tavern, the members of the Committee included Robert Carter Nicholas, Bland, Benjamin Harrison, Pendleton, Dudley Digges and Archibald Cary. Then December, 1773, brought the Boston Tea Party. Headlong the decade of crisis rushed toward its climax.

5

"The Art of Being Honest"

PARLIAMENT ordered the Port of Boston closed on June 1, 1774. The shortsighted attitude of George III and his ministers seemed to imply that what occurred in Massachusetts should be no concern in Virginia, and for men who appeared possessed with a mania for piling one lamentable blunder upon another it became difficult to sort out the degree of tragedy that should be attached to each. In Williamsburg on May twenty-fourth the House of Burgesses resolved that "with Apprehension of the great Dangers, to be derived to British America, from the hostile Invasion of the City of Boston, in our Sister Colony of Massachusetts Bay" the first of June should become "a Day of Fasting, Humiliation, and Prayer." Members of the House were asked "devoutly to implore the Divine Interposition, for averting the heavy Calamity which threatens Destruction to our civil Rights, and the Evils of civil War." How far Virginia already had effected "the real American Revolution" was reflected in the declaration that this action was taken "to give us one Heart and one Mind firmly to oppose, by all just and proper Means, every Injury to *American* Rights." In trusting that "the Minds of his Majesty and his Parliament, may be inspired from above with Wisdom, Moderation, and Justice, to remove from the loyal People of *America* all Cause of Danger, from a continued Pursuit of Measures, pregnant with their Ruin," the core of the crisis was laid bare. Edmund Burke would understand and one day cry, "We cannot, I fear, falsify the pedigree of this fierce people, and persuade them that they are not sprung from a nation in whose veins the blood of freedom circulates."

Governor Dunmore reacted as everyone expected, dissolving the Assembly two days later for a resolve "conceived in such Terms as reflect highly upon his Majesty and the Parliament of *Great Britain*." With a gift that equalled Burke's for speaking his mind succinctly, Jefferson might have replied then, as he wrote later, "The King's argument is with God—not with us!" On the appointed day the burgesses attended Bruton Parish Church and the Reverend Mr. Price preached, as instructed, "a Sermon, suitable to the Occasion."

In August, looking toward the meeting next month of the First Continental Congress in Philadelphia, Virginia elected as its delegates Peyton Randolph, Patrick Henry, George Washington, Richard Henry Lee, Richard Bland, Benjamin Harrison, and Edmund Pendleton. Confined by illness to his home in Charlottesville, Jefferson chafed at missing these sessions in Williamsburg. His mind was filled with ideas he wished to place before the Virginia delegates, and with an indefatigable will that was the essence of the man he wrote a long and thoughtful document to be read aloud. On a hot summer day the Virginia patriots gathered to hear Peyton Randolph read Jefferson's suggestions. With fire, with eloquence, they heard Jefferson warn George III:

"Open your breast Sire, to liberal and expanded thought. Let not the name of George the third be a blot in the page of history."

The mind that had been tutored under Wythe spoke with brilliance:

"The whole art of government consists in the art of being honest."

On his mountaintop, looking across forests that rolled like the sea, Jefferson wrote with a mind soaring like the eagles above the beautiful highlands he loved:

"The god who gave us life, gave us liberty at the same time: the hand of force may destroy, but cannot disjoin them."

Grievance by grievance—the pattern of the Declaration of Independence—Jefferson stated the case against George III. The restrictions that had been placed on trade, the repeated instances of unfair taxes, the suspension in New York of the legislature, the refusal for trifling reason of royal assent to necessary laws, the dissolution of representative bodies of government for endeavoring to perform their duty in good conscience, the apparent effort to take from the people the right of representation, the sending of armed troops to the colonies, even the wounding of human rights by permitting greedy corsairs to impose the institution of slavery on the colonies at a time when they were too young to resist such an infamous practice—all these were arguments that Jefferson placed on the record with force of mind and passion of heart. Peyton Randolph read well, an experienced parliamentarian; Jefferson gave him vigorous sentences to articulate:

> . . . And the wretched criminal, if he happen to have offended on the American side, stripped of his privilege of trial by peers, of his vicinage, removed from the place where alone full evidence could be obtained, without money, without counsel, without friends, without exculpatory proof, is tried before judges predetermined to condemn. The cowards who would suffer a countryman to be torn from the bowels of their society in order to be thus offered a sacrifice of parliamentary tyranny, would merit that everlasting infamy now fixed on the authors of the act!

Again Peyton Randolph read:

> . . . his majesty has no right to land a single armed man on our shores; and those whom he sends here are liable to our laws for the suppression and punish-

ment of Riots, Routs, and unlawful assemblies, or are hostile bodies invading us in defiance of law.

Again:

> . . . his Majesty has expressly made the civil subordinate to the military. But can his majesty thus put down all law under his feet? Can he erect a power superior to that which erected himself? He has done it indeed by force; but let him remember that force cannot give right.

Those who listened, not agreeing on every point, here and there wincing at an acid phrase, respected Jefferson's right to be heard and voted that the document should be published. As *A Summary View of the Rights of British America,* the pamphlet made Jefferson famous at home and abroad. A copy, coming into the hands of the astute Burke, had enormous impact upon this man who came to believe that "in no country perhaps in the world is the law so general a study." Jefferson's arguments shook Parliament with a heated debate; but the reply known as "Lord North's Proposals" that ultimately evolved from this searching of the British soul revealed how little had been learned.

But if the British must insist that an irresistible logic forced their course, in the colonies an irresistible logic in 1774 brought delegates to Philadelphia for the First Continental Congress. Here, as president, Peyton Randolph would hear Patrick Henry (and no one knew him better or what to expect) proclaim that through British oppression "we were reduced to a State of Nature." He conceived of himself, said Henry, not as "a Virginian but an American." The crisis now had run almost its full cycle, and the man who held the gavel and the men who held the floor had become comrades in thought and would soon become comrades in arms.

In late March, 1775, the Virginia Assembly, meeting in Richmond at St. John's Church, voted to assemble and train the militia; Lord Dunmore on the night of the twentieth of April ordered marines from a British frigate to run off with the gunpowder in the Magazine at Williamsburg; the day before a skirmish was fought between colonists and British troops at Lexington. "The sword is now drawn," proclaimed the *Virginia Gazette,* reporting the battles at Lexington and Concord, "and God knows when it will be sheathed."

So the crisis that began on a May day in 1765 led, grudging step by grudging step, to another May day in 1776 when after one hundred and fifty-seven years a noble chapter ended in the history of representative government. Read the minutes for May sixth: "Several Members met, but did neither proceed to Business, nor adjourn, as a House of Burgesses. FINIS." On May fifteenth 1776 the Virginia Convention unanimously adopted a resolution directing its delegates at the Continental Congress to move that the united colonies declare themselves free and independent states. At Waller's Grove next day Williamsburg celebrated the new freedom symbolized by the Grand Union Flag of the American colonies spanking in the breeze above the cupola of the Capitol; salutes of cannon, brilliant displays of fireworks added to the gaiety as toasts were offered to "the Grand Congress of the United States" and "to General Washington—victory to the American arms!" On the seventeenth the doors of Bruton Parish Church stood open for a day of fasting and prayer, and those who made their way to this fine old chapel passed splendidly frocked gentlemen from the Tidewater plantations and the homespun-clad, bold-eyed "wild Irish" who had come from settlements beyond the Blue Ridge. Possibly they passed without special notice a quiet man who showed the strain of his long journey, for George Mason had left a sick bed to face the responsibility awaiting him in Williamsburg.

The first George Mason had reached Virginia some time after 1651, and soon was settled in the rich lowlands of the Northern Neck. The present George Mason, the fourth to bear the name, inherited an estate that had grown to approximately five thousand acres, and in the tradition of the family managed the plantation with care, wisdom and profit; but an inheritance that he considered of equal significance was his uncle's library of fifteen hundred volumes. Perhaps one-third of these books were on legal subjects, and although George Mason was always a competent consultant on the law, he never sought a license as an attorney. Yet that fact was in character for a man who liked to call himself "a private gentleman" and both looked and lived the part. Trustee of Alexandria, justice of the Fairfax County Court, vestryman of Truro Parish were offices in local government that George Mason filled in good conscience and good humor. A resplendent figure, Mason appeared in his brown velvet jacket and yellow waistcoat with lace ruffles trimming his blouse at neck and wrists and a dark wig emphasizing fine brown eyes and a sloping, scholarly forehead.

No man in Virginia was more devoted to family than George Mason; when he built a new home he insisted that there must be a window to light the beds of each of his nine children, and when in 1773 his wife died, intimate friends like George Washington heard him speak of "the duty I owe to a poor little helpless family of orphans to whom I must act the part of Father and Mother both."

In 1759 he made the long journey to Williamsburg with Washington to take his seat as a new member of the House of Burgesses. It was not a happy experience, and later he confessed to Washington: "Mere vexation and disgust threw me into such an ill state of health that before the Convention rose, I was sometimes near fainting in the House." The advice he gave to his sons was to beware of the shams of politics. After one term in the House he preferred keeping in the background and helping his friend Washington by drafting important resolutions. Poor health also influenced George Mason to shun public life. A man who often was plagued by a convulsive colic that left him unable to keep on his stomach more than a mild milk punch well might recoil from the prospect of the hard, dusty coach ride, the indifferent meals and the even more indifferent beds in rural hostelries that were suffered by those who bridged the comforts between Williamsburg and the Northern Neck.

Yet once "the very real Revolution" became both a fact of mind and a bleeding reality of battle, Virginia called on this sickly, oft-times nettlesome scholar-planter-aristocrat, knowing that years of study and reflection had given him a keen insight into the functions and obligations of government. A "smart fit of the gout" explained why he had been delayed from attending earlier the session of the Convention. A copy of the resolution proposing independence that already had been adopted came into his hands. As he might have expected, it was no labor of profound intelligence.

George Mason pursed his lips and thought. Along Duke of Gloucester Street rumbled the splendid coach of a planter's family; he glimpsed within ladies in feathers and elegant silks. In the taverns the wild Irish from across the Blue Ridge tried eating with forks and sometimes went back to fingers that licked easier. At Market Square he saw frontiersmen leaning on squirrel guns—to them a far more useful instrument of government than the ballot box—and he saw as well, standing by themselves and viewing with suspicious eyes the dandies in velvets and satins, that peculiar breed of man called the Pennsylvania Dutch. The clannish Germans, the Scotch who liked being clergymen and schoolmasters and Indian fighters . . . all types, all classes, all manner of American customs bumped elbows here in Williamsburg, and, not unreasonably, the question they posed in George Mason's mind was how to knock their heads together and persuade them to agree on a fair and workable plan of government.

George Mason re-read the resolutions proposing independence. The timid preamble was not to the taste of this liberal Anglican who exemplified so well the dominant force of this decade of crisis when free thought produced the free state. He accepted membership on the committee appointed to draw up a plan of government, discovering, as he was by no means reticent in growling, that it was "overcharged with useless members." Gout-ridden, irritable, he did not look forward to the coming days in Williamsburg with any sense of cheer: "We shall, in all probability, have a thousand ridiculous and impractical proposals, and of course a plan formed of heterogeneous, jarring and unintelligible ingredients."

Under George Mason's leadership, nothing of the sort occurred. By June he would be ready to present to the Convention a "Declaration of Rights" so basic as a cornerstone of American democracy that the first ten amendments to the Constitution are based on it. In after years, realizing the stature of the work, George Mason said in somewhat better mood: "We seem to have been treading on enchanted ground." And in enchanted language and thought Mason's "Declaration of Rights" proclaimed:

> . . . all men are created equally free and independent, and have certain inherent natural rights, of which they cannot, by any compact, deprive or divest their posterity; among which are the enjoyment of life and liberty, with the means of acquiring and possessing property, and pursuing and obtaining happiness and safety.

No aspect of government among free men could George Mason touch without endowing it with eloquence and a rich and glowing vitality. Whence came the power to govern, except from God and nature, so that government must exist for the "common benefit, protection, and security of the people, nation, or community." No man deserved special privilege; no officer or judge should derive power through heredity; and powers of government should be kept separated so that one group made laws for another to administer and a third to judge their fairness.

To Mason it was a cardinal rule that "No free government can be preserved but . . . by frequent recurrence to fundamental principles." The sensitivity, the wisdom, the character of this man who sought through the "Declaration of Rights" to give to Virginia and America principles that would serve the spirit, the will, the needs of all the people, shines through his legacy to his dearly loved sons when "on a father's blessing" he charged them "never to let the motives of private interest or ambition induce them to betray, nor the terrors of poverty and disgrace, or the fear of danger or of death, deter them from asserting the liberty of their country and endeavoring to transmit to their posterity those sacred rights to which themselves were born." In the "Declaration of Rights," as though "on a father's blessing," Mason charged Virginia to protect "those sacred rights" of elections held openly, honestly, and freely; of laws that could never be suspended without the consent of the people or their representatives; of the ancient custom of trial by jury. Into the word freedom he breathed life and created dimension. Only a despotic government ever could wish to destroy the freedom of the press, "one of the great bulwarks of liberty"; and whereas war demanded armies, in times of peace he saw standing armies as probably "dangerous to liberty" and, under all circumstances, declared that the supreme authority must rest with the representatives of the people and not the generals or the admirals.

But freedom was something more—an intellectual concept, true; but also a body of emotions, a quality of personal being—so that people to be free must be by nature firmly just, moderate and temperate, respectful of frugality and virtue. In a round script Mason's pen conveyed the ideas that arose as he found himself "treading on enchanted ground." In religion, "the duty we owe our Creator," he pleaded that men act "only by reason and conviction, not by force or violence" since for men who worshiped according to conscience "it is the mutual duty of all to practise Christian forbearance, love, charity towards each other." In such lofty thoughts George Mason, expecting to contend with "a thousand ridiculous and impractical proposals," achieved his masterpiece. The planter from the Tidewater, the up-country farmer, the frontiersman from the mountain, debated it before the Convention for two weeks and found only slight changes or additions to make. On June twelfth the Convention voted unanimously to adopt it. Quietly George Mason went home and for too long history ignored this true architect of modern American democracy.

By courier a copy of Virginia's "Declaration of Rights" was carried to Philadelphia where a well-known "son" of Williamsburg had rented the second floor of a new brick house at 230 High Street for thirty-five shillings a week. Here through the hot summer of 1776, Jefferson toiled at a folding desk and glanced down, in contemplative moments, upon sprawling, panting Philadelphia. With John Adams, Benjamin Franklin, Roger Sherman and Robert R. Livingston, Jefferson had been selected by the Continental Congress to draw up a declaration of independence.

"I was delighted with its high tone and the flights of oratory with which it abounded," John Adams recalled, testifying that it had been no idle choice that the author of *A Summary View* had been asked to draft this document. Adams asserted that he "certainly never would oppose" the passage concerning Negro slavery, "which though I knew his Southern brethren would never suffer to pass in Congress." Jefferson, while admitting the clause "reprobating the enslaving [of] the inhabitants of Africa" was struck out to mollify South Carolina and Georgia, added: "Our Northern brethren also I believe felt a little tender under those censures; for tho' their people have very few slaves themselves yet they had been pretty considerable carriers of them to others."

When Jefferson's draft of the document was read to the committee, Adams did not remember that "Franklin or Sherman criticized any thing" and Jefferson's own recollection was that the alterations proposed by Franklin and Adams "were two or three only, and merely verbal." For his own part, Adams said, he would not have called the king a tyrant, adding "I thought this too personal; for I never believed George to be a tyrant in disposition and in nature; I always believed him to be deceived by his courtiers on both sides of the Atlantic, and in his official capacity only, cruel." Jefferson was too passionate, too much given to scolding; still Adams wouldn't stand on the point: "We were all in haste. Congress was impatient, and the instrument was reported, as I believe, in Jefferson's handwriting."

For three days Congress debated the Declaration of Independence, and Jefferson's annoyance still lingered in his *Autobiography:* "The pusillanimous idea that we had friends in England worth keeping terms with, still haunted the minds of many. For this reason those passages which conveyed censures on the people of England were struck out, lest they should give them offence." The debate on the slavery clause followed and that, too, was deleted. Yet the great body of Jefferson's document endured, the rich, vigorous, flowing magic of Jefferson's language remained, transforming prose into poetry—"We hold these truths to be self-evident, that all men are created equal, that they are endowed by their Creator with certain unalienable Rights" . . . "Governments are instituted among Men, deriving their just powers from the consent of the governed" . . . "But when a long train of abuses and usurpations, pursuing invariably the same Object evinces a design to reduce them under absolute

Despotism, it is their right, it is their duty, to throw off such Government, and to provide new Guards for their future security."

So did the decade of crisis end. The words were Jefferson's—words, truly, that rolled like the highlands at Charlottesville, where green forests crested on smoky blue mountains. But the ideas had come from many minds—here echoing an early heresy of Richard Henry Lee, Patrick Henry and John Fleming; again crystalizing the love of order, the respect for an authority that must be worthy of respect which had been the essence of being to Wythe and Bland and Pendleton; now reflecting the steadfastness of principle (indeed, as Burke insisted, of basically English principle) that was dearer than life or fortune to Washington and Peyton Randolph and others who deserve mention in a full chronicle of that brilliant age of the great amateurs; then breathing the eloquent spirit of George Mason who would charge his sons never to forsake "those sacred rights to which themselves were born."

"The very real Revolution" had ended and the war commenced. Washington's diaries break off abruptly on June 19, 1775, four days after Congress unanimously elected him general and commander-in-chief of all the forces raised, or to be raised, by the united colonies.

When he resumes his journal the month is May, the year 1781, and events have been unleashed that carry this story of America back to the point whence it started—to Jamestown and Williamsburg and Yorktown.

YORKTOWN

Triumph of Faith

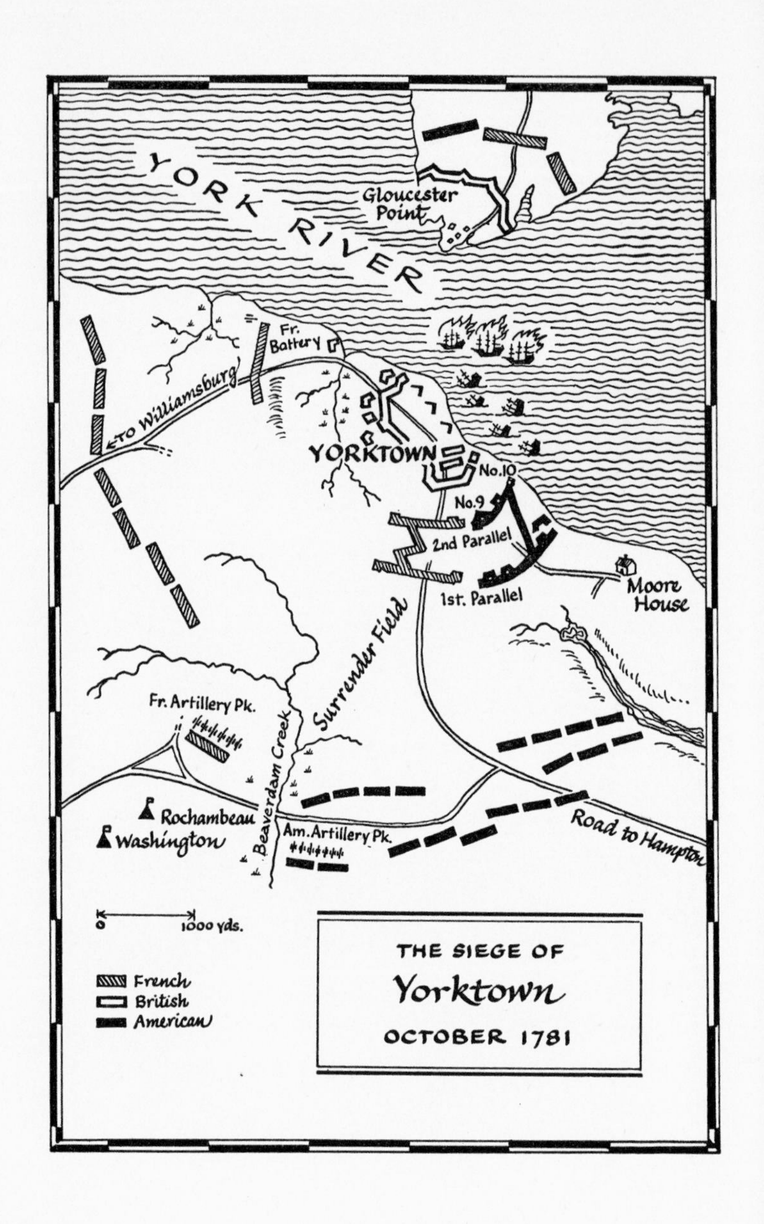
YORK RIVER
Gloucester Point
Fr. Battery
To Williamsburg
YORKTOWN
No. 10
No. 9
2nd Parallel
1st. Parallel
Moore House
Surrender Field
Fr. Artillery Pk.
Beaverdam Creek
Rochambeau
Washington
Am. Artillery Pk.
Road to Hampton
0
1000 yds.
French
British
American
THE SIEGE OF
Yorktown
OCTOBER 1781

6

From the Hudſon to the York

ON May 22, 1781 five generals met in the pleasant little town of Wethersfield, Connecticut. General Washington, accompanied by Generals Knox and Duportail, had a force of thirty-five hundred Continentals quartered on the Hudson around West Point; and Comte de Rochambeau, accompanied by the Chevalier de Chastellux, had journeyed from Newport, Rhode Island where a corps of four thousand French effectives was encamped. Like a curious, sniffing dog, spring had begun to explore the Connecticut Valley, but for the careworn Washington, burdened with the responsibility of new decisions, the season was more like March in Virginia.

Six years had passed since last Washington had visited Mount Vernon, more than four hundred miles to the southward. During that interval the lines in Washington's face had deepened, his mouth had tended to grow firmer, his smile more fleeting, his eyes more thoughtful. The marks were understandable. In this age of the great amateurs, when the dependence of the military on the civil system was a basic tenet, Washington had learned well the stresses inherent in dealing both with the nature of war and the nature of human nature. His authority had been derived from a Continental Congress that exercised at best a shadowy sort of central authority; his effectiveness, however, largely rested with state governments that co-operated if they felt so inclined and then, very likely, at a snail's pace. The situation was one to vex a Job, and Washington confessed limits of patience. Often troubled and angered, he poured out his heart in the pages of his journal and before leaving for Wethersfield his complaints had been many:

> Instead of having Magazines filled with provisions, we have a scanty pittance scattered here and there in the different States. Instead of having our Arsenals well supplied with Military Stores, they are poorly provided, and the Workmen all leaving them. . . . Instead of having a regular System of transportation established upon credit—or funds in the Qr. Master's hands to defray the contingent expences of it we have neither the one nor the other and all that business, or a great part of it, being done by Military Impress, we are daily and hourly oppressing the people—souring their tempers—and alienating their affections. Instead of having the Regiments compleated to the new establishment . . . scarce any State in the Union has, at this hour, an eighth part of its quota in

> the field . . . and instead of having the prospect of a glorious offensive campaign before us, we have a bewildered and gloomy defensive one—unless we should receive a powerful aid of Ships—Land Troops and Money from our generous allies . . .

A prospect, Washington added, "too contingent to build upon." Yet confession was good for Washington's soul; riding to Wethersfield to meet Rochambeau and Chastellux, he rebounded from old adversities with new ideas. This vitality in Washington symbolized the strength in the American rebellion that baffled the British. The years 1776 and 1777 had found England taking the war in dead earnest, driving the Americans off Long Island, capturing New York, and setting the stage a year later to capture Philadelphia. With (the British hoped) the central states overawed, Burgoyne marched down from the St. Lawrence to seize Albany, control the Hudson, and sever New England from the remainder of the country. Instead Burgoyne walked into a trap; unsupported in the forest, he surrendered, and by the close of 1778 the astonishing Americans under Washington virtually had bottled up the British in New York.

Failure in the north produced effort in the south, and therein, for all its oversimplification, still resided the essence of the war as Washington traveled to Wethersfield in 1781. And, looking squarely at the military situation, the essential elements were that the Continental position in the South looked the weakest and the British position in New York the most vulnerable. In military arithmetic one added to one invariably produced alternative courses, and Washington proceeded to enumerate them. If he combined Rochambeau's forces with his own and moved against the British in New York, the desirable result should be either (1) to win the city and its garrison or (2) to give it such a thumping scare that British detachments would be recalled from the South, thus reducing the pressure on Greene in the Carolinas and on Lafayette in Virginia. What support the French fleet might lend was not a part of the Wethersfield plan; perhaps the French ships could move from the Carribbean in time to be of help against New York but the prospect was otherwise.

The plan that Washington devised in late May bore very little resemblance to the plan he would have in late August, for his mind responded quickly to event and resulted in an achievement as brilliant as any upon which his military fame rests. In the end the decision to move from the Hudson to the York would be reached and, considering the distance and the risk, would represent elasticity at its best. Meanwhile at Wethersfield the more limited objective alone made sense.

Rochambeau hurried back to Newport, and Washington, remaining an extra day in Wethersfield, fell to the weary toil of letterwriting. He urged the governors of New England to alert their militia to be ready to move on a week's notice; and, since hope could be infectious, urged as well that they show liberality in supplying provisions, powder, wagons. To the Chevalier de la Luzerne, French Minister at Philadelphia, he wrote of the importance in encouraging De Grasse to bring the French fleet to the American coast in time to support the projected offensive operations. Thereafter he was forced to wait in this age when it required a month for a letter from Greene to reach Washington, and ten days for a letter from Lafayette to come into his hands.

Late May also brought climactic changes to the war in the south. After Cowpens and Guilford Court House, where battles won amounted to campaigns lost, Earl Cornwallis was in one of those moods between belligerency and sulk where he had definitely decided that the war had better be run his way if it was going to be won. "If we mean an offensive war in America, we must abandon New York and bring our whole force into Virginia," Cornwallis wrote General Phillips, indulging in his old habit of saving his best surprises for his colleagues. Otherwise Cornwallis favored scrapping a southern campaign; or, in the colorful phrase that he never seemed to lack, the British might as well "stick to our salt pork at New York, sending now and then a detachment to steal tobacco, etc." Whatever General Phillips thought of these opinions was of mere academic interest to Cornwallis, who, without waiting for a reply, cast off the plague the Carolinas had become by marching the two hundred and twenty-three miles to the Appomattox River. Phillips had died of a bilious fever so that Benedict Arnold greeted Cornwallis at Petersburg on a bright May twentieth. Arnold's guile doubtless covered not making too sharp an inquiry into what plan Cornwallis had devised for his Virginia campaign. The answer, frankly, was none at all.

Twenty-three miles away at Richmond that day, commanding some three thousand Continentals and militia, Lafayette shared with Arnold the guessing game as to Cornwallis's intentions. At Charlottesville to the northwest von Steuben played his own shrewd game of cussing in three languages while training another five hundred raw Continentals. Wayne and the Pennsylvania Line had not yet left York, but Lafayette counted on Mad Anthony's appearance (sooner, he hoped, than later). A letter going to Clinton in New York revealed Cornwallis thinking as he fought, somewhat fretfully. He would now proceed, said Cornwallis as though the job was as good as done, "to dislodge Lafayette from Richmond and with my light troops to destroy any magazines or stores in the neighborhood." Clearly looking to his own comfort, Cornwallis then proposed "to move to the Neck of Williamsburg, which is represented as healthy and where some subsistence may be procured, and keep myself unengaged from operations which might interfere with your plan for the campaign, until I have the satisfaction of hearing from you."

Lafayette kept his wits. As he wrote Washington, he was "not strong enough even to get beaten." He dropped back seventy miles to Ely's Ford on the Rapidan, waiting for Wayne to join him. Cornwallis lost interest in chasing Lafayette at about the North Anna, and sent a detachment under Tarleton to bag that rascal Jefferson, now governor of Virginia and an old thorn in the side of the British; another detachment under Simcoe was sent to put a finish to Steuben's drilling. Jefferson escaped and Steuben managed to reach Lafayette. Thoroughly frustrated, Cornwallis marched through Richmond for Williamsburg.

Busy with preparations for the operation against New York, Washington received letters from Virginia on June 4, 7 and 11. Cornwallis appeared to be carrying everything before him in Virginia, and Jefferson urged Washington either to send or to bring in person relief to his home state. But Admiral De Grasse also had been writing a letter, dated March twenty-ninth "at sea," saying that from the West Indies he would sail for North America, though he doubted if the fleet would arrive earlier than July fifteenth. At what place he appeared made little difference to the admiral; he could not long linger, however, and everything should be in readiness for an operation. Rochambeau received De Grasse's communication on June ninth and relayed its contents to Washington on the thirteenth, who, understandably, considered the news "very interesting." In replying, Rochambeau explained the details of the Wethersfield plan to De Grasse and suggested that he "enter the Chesapeake on his way, as there might be an opportunity of striking an important stroke there, and then to proceed immediately to New York, and be ready to co-operate with the allied armies in an attack upon that city." This intelligence sped to De Grasse aboard the frigate *Concorde.*

Events had moved along in Virginia and on June twenty-fifth Cornwallis entered Williamsburg. St. George Tucker, an officer in the Virginia militia and a resident of the city, was filled with the indignities of the occupation. A letter to his wife described how life had changed in Williamsburg after Cornwallis and his redcoats

> . . . remained for some Days, and with them Pestilence and Famine took root, and Poverty brought up the Rear. Instead of attempting a florid Description of the Horrors of this Place, I will endeavour to give you an Account of the Situations of a few Individuals with whom you are acquainted. Our Friend *Madison* and his Lady (they have lost their Son) were turned out of their House [the President's House] to make Room for Lord *Cornwallis.* Happily the College afforded them an Asylum. They were refused the

> small Privilege of drawing Water from their own Well. A contemptuous Treatment, with the Danger of starving were the only Evils he recounted, as none of his Servants left him. . . . The Smallpox, which the hellish Polling of these infamous Wretches has spread in every Place through which they have passed has now obtained a Crisis throughout the Place so that there is scarcely a Person to be found to nurse those who are most afflicted by it. . . . To add to the Catalogue of Mortifications, they constrained all the Inhabitants of the Town to take Paroles.

With plundering and famine, with sickness and the confiscation of slaves, a swarm of flies followed Cornwallis into Williamsburg and added to the city's torment. The British lingered ten days, long enough to seem a lifetime. If Cornwallis appeared irritable, neither the flies nor the hostile residents of Williamsburg deserved the blame. A vexed Clinton in New York had ordered Cornwallis to send part of his force north, which meant withdrawing from Williamsburg, crossing the James and marching to Portsmouth, the point of embarkation.

A watchful Lafayette had set up headquarters at Tyree's Plantation about twenty miles away, and was rather like a high-spirited puppy with his patrol and picket line constantly nipping at British heels. Ebenezer Denny caught the essence of those ten days: "Pennsylvania troops retreat —advance again. See the Marquis' light troops but seldom —know they are not far off. Kept constantly on the move." The Fourth of July came and Ebenezer Wild described how the Americans celebrated the anniversary of their independence with "a fu de joy [feu de joie] fired by the whole army (except those on duty), after which the Light Infantry was manoeuvered by Major Read on a plain before the Marquis's quarters."

Along the narrow road to Jamestown that same day Cornwallis marched from Williamsburg with his head filled with schemes (and all of them good) for making a fool out of Lafayette. The British force with Cornwallis numbered about four thousand, and Lafayette's troops, including Wayne's Pennsylvania line and the Virginia militia, approximated forty-five hundred. The advantage of experience leaned more toward the redcoats than the rebels. Yet, with Lafayette, in addition to Wayne and von Steuben, were such seasoned commanders as Richard Butler, William Campbell, and Peter Muhlenberg. Cornwallis had not kept his patrols busy during the past ten days without learning these facts. Moreover, in taking his army across the river at Jamestown, Cornwallis reasonably could anticipate that Lafayette would make some sort of attack upon the rear. In high spirits a letter informed Clinton: "If I can get a favourable opportunity of striking a blow at him without loss of time, I will certainly try it."

Cornwallis baited a clever trap. Between Jamestown and Green Spring for a distance of about three miles of

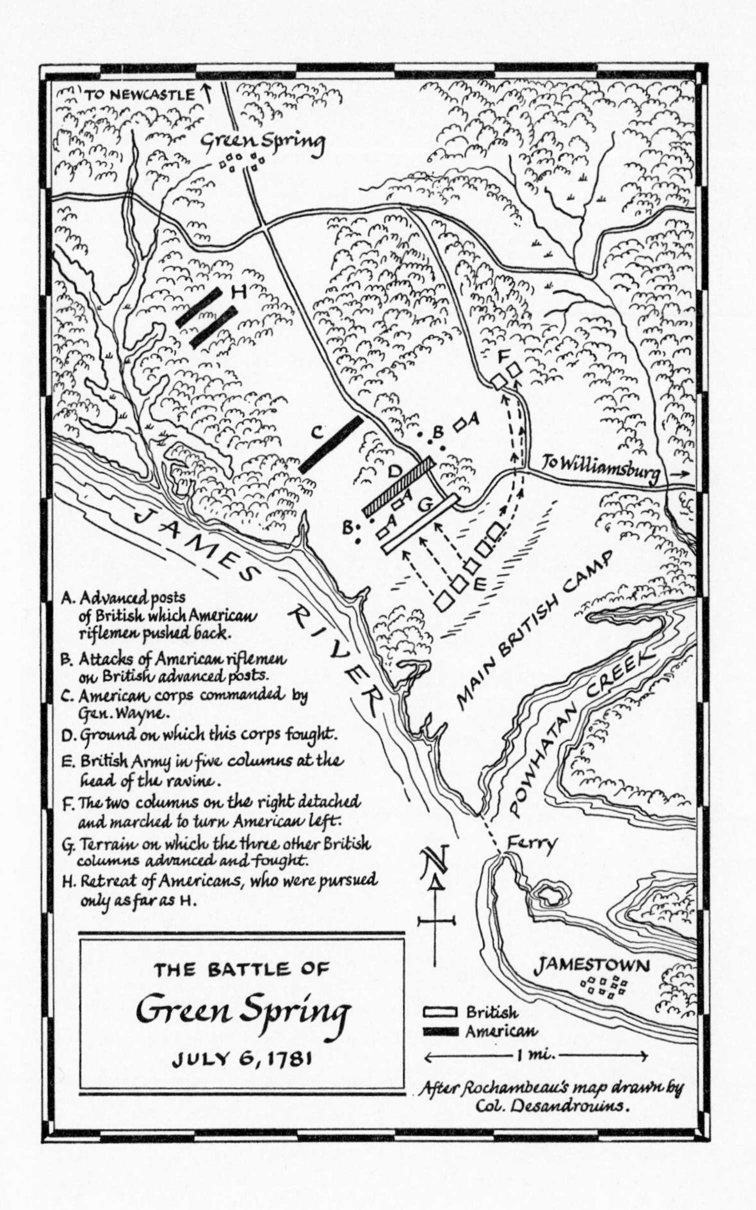
TO NEWCASTLE
Green Spring
H
C
B
A
D
A
G
B.
A
E
F
To Williamsburg
JAMES RIVER
MAIN BRITISH CAMP
POWHATAN CREEK
Ferry
N
JAMESTOWN
A. Advanced posts of British which American riflemen pushed back.
B. Attacks of American riflemen on British advanced posts.
C. American corps commanded by Gen. Wayne.
D. Ground on which this corps fought.
E. British Army in five columns at the head of the ravine.
F. The two columns on the right detached and marched to turn American left.
G. Terrain on which the three other British columns advanced and fought.
H. Retreat of Americans, who were pursued only as far as H.
THE BATTLE OF
Green Spring
JULY 6, 1781
British
American
1 mi.
After Rochambeau's map drawn by Col. Desandrouins.

alternating marsh, wood and cultivated fields the road to Jamestown traversed a skimpy causeway. Beyond the marsh and between Powhatan Creek and the James rose an area of high ground called the "Maine." Cornwallis chose the east side of the "Maine" to set up his camp—with malice in his heart as far as Lafayette was concerned. On his left flank toward the Williamsburg Road he placed the veteran Queen's Rangers under Simcoe; on the right the wily Tarleton watched the Jamestown Road above Glass House Point. Cornwallis could consider his army well posted, not only to protect all movements but also for those delicate moments when in the face of superior American forces the last small body of British troops must fall back to Jamestown Island.

Tarleton had been well supplied with money—to which he could, if he liked, add "encouraging promises"—for the purpose of buying off "informants" who, circulating among the Americans, were to spread false reports that the major portion of the British army already had crossed the James. Then on July sixth, under orders from Cornwallis, a British cavalry patrol on contacting the Americans retreated across the causeway to the "Maine"; and to make the withdrawal of the cavalry seem even more convincing evidence that the enemy was not in force, British riflemen came up to supply a cover. At the same time these pickets kept the Americans from crossing the marsh to the "Maine," where they could discover that Cornwallis had concealed his army at the head of a ravine with stern instruction to keep out of sight until called for.

For good reason then, in the telling phrase of Lieutenant Balneaves of the 80th Regiment, Cornwallis allowed his "picquets to be insulted"; for the same reason part of the army under Simcoe had been sent across the river to stage a series of dress parades creating the illusion that the British occupied the south shore of the James in great numbers. Such, in the main, was the setting for the smart, heated skirmish sometimes dignified with the title of the Battle of Green Spring. About two o'clock on the afternoon of July sixth Wayne came up "to reconnoitre with a *Military Eye*" and perhaps to listen with an unmilitary ear to exaggerated reports concerning the size of the British withdrawal across the James. The musket fire grew momentarily brisker; when it ended "near sun-set" Wayne would be under no delusions concerning the situation he had encountered.

Lafayette guessed sooner. The contradictory reports awakened his caution. He observed Simcoe's extravagant parading across the river and surmised that it was a ruse. Lafayette hastened to Green Spring, eager to pull back his forces, but before the Marquis could reach the field Cornwallis played the trump in his sprightly game of duplicity. A British fieldpiece had been set up to fire upon the Americans, then to cease firing as though to indicate a British "retreat." The decoy worked to perfection—the Americans came up and the redcoats moved out of the ravine to engage them. What resulted, in the impassioned opinion of one Pennsylvanian, was "*Madness!* Mad A——y, by G—, I never knew such a piece of work heard of—about eight hundred troops opposed to five or six thousand veterans upon their own ground."

As, indeed, they were. Lafayette ordered Wayne to retreat, placing him, Mad Anthony commented, "among a *Choice of Difficulties.*" His best defense, he decided, was to advance and charge the British, which his Pennsylvanians did "with such vivacity as to produce the desired effect i. e., checking them in their advance & diverting [them] from their first Manoeuver"—a considerable understatement since Wayne had faced the imminent danger of having both flanks turned. To Denny the picture of those moments became unforgetable:

> Saw the British light infantry, distinctly, advancing at arm's-length distance, and their second line in close order, with shouldered musket . . . My captain, Montgomery, received a shot in his foot and had hopped back in the rear; Lieutenant Bluer being absent, the charge of the company devolved on me; young and inexperienced, exhausted with hunger and fatigue, had like to have disgraced myself—had eat

> nothing all day but a few backberries—was faint, and with difficulty kept my place; once or twice was about to throw away my arms (a very heavy espontoon). The company were almost all old soldiers. . . .

Knowing how to handle their muskets, the veterans saw the British waver and stop. This was the moment Wayne wanted to order a retreat. Lafayette posted the light infantry to cover the movement. Not to expect, under the circumstances, such a withdrawal to end in headlong flight was to expect soldiers to act like insects. Wayne bemoaned the "many brave & worthy Officers & soldiers killed & wounded"; nor was he cheered to have two of his three fieldpieces fall into British hands. Order at length was restored at Green Spring and later that night, withdrawing to Norrell's Mill and Chickahominy Church, Lafayette was strengthened by a juncture with the militia under Brigadier General Robert Lawson.

Next morning Tarleton led two hundred dragoons and eighty mounted infantry across the swamp in a pursuit that carried about four miles before a brush with a cavalry patrol turned him back to the British camp. Cornwallis congratulated himself on a victory—he had held the field—and, as a British officer brightly observed, the fact that several Americans had been "wounded in the lower extremities" gave "proof that the young soldiers had taken good aim." By nightfall on July seventh Cornwallis completed crossing the James, leaving for future speculation what new pattern the campaign in Virginia might take.

On that bloody sixth of July when Cornwallis was outwitting the Americans at Green Spring, uneasy moments plagued Washington along the Hudson. On June twenty-fourth Washington had camped near Peekskill, waiting for Rochambeau. By the twenty-eighth he saw no reason why he shouldn't start operations with a surprise attack on the British forts at the north end of New York Island. On July second eight hundred troops were sent down the river in boats while Washington planned to march the remainder of his army to within supporting distance of these forces. Rochambeau could catch up to him later.

The expedition, for all that it involved one brisk little scurry with the British, was a fizzle from start to finish. The timing, an old bugaboo in such military schemes, failed at virtually all points. Washington was more than happy to fall back on Dobbs Ferry, where on July sixth Rochambeau finally joined him. Yet the psychological results were considerable. Clinton's jitters were nowhere better reflected than in Virginia where poor Cornwallis, trying to live through the irritabilities of a muggy July, contended with conflicting orders that would have sent him, variously, to New York, Philadelphia, New York again, Yorktown, and Old Point Comfort. So the pawns moved, the kings castled, the queens and rooks and bishops shifted positions in this chess game played on a board that reached from the Hudson to the York.

The next two moves, however, were decisive. Clinton decided about the twentieth of July that Cornwallis needed to settle somewhere, would have preferred Old Point Comfort and had to be content with Cornwallis's choice of Yorktown. By the twenty-second of August the British had occupied this delightful town with its high bluffs and protecting swamps. The other move was Washington's, and the event that motivated it was another letter from De Grasse that Rochambeau received on August fourteenth. The admiral announced that on the thirteenth he would sail directly for Chesapeake Bay, preferring an action there over New York. Washington's journal entry revealed a mind that could adjust to realities:

> Matters having now come to a crisis, and a decisive plan to be determined on, I was obliged, from the shortness of Count de Grasses promised stay on this Coast, the apparent disinclination of their Naval Officers to force the harbour of New York and the feeble compliance of the States to my requisitions for Men, hitherto, and little prospect of greater exertion in the future, to give up all idea of attacking New York; and instead thereof to remove the French Troops and a detachment from the American Army to the Head of Elk to be transported to Virginia for the purpose of co-operating with the force from the West Indies against the Troops in that State.

Should the casting of the "net" at Yorktown that ultimately caught Cornwallis be called "a piece of blind fortune?" Every student of the Virginia campaign and of Washington's position among military leaders must grapple with this question; and few excel Henry P. Johnston in answering with penetrating insight: "His perfect understanding of the situation at the moment it was time to act, and his prompt decision to act as he did, prove the high order of his military talents. It was by the exercise of the same qualities that he executed his memorable retreat from Long Island in 1776, and, again, turned upon Trenton four months later. The present campaign, like all before it, was pre-eminently shaped by circumstances. If the commander-in-chief was only in part instrumental in shaping them, he watched, and at the right instant turned them to account."*

Five days after learning of De Grasse's intention, Washington moved. Watching from New York, Clinton thought, not unreasonably, that Washington had returned to New Jersey to play the old game of coming at New York through a feint toward Staten Island. This belief was precisely what Washington wished Clinton to hold when on the morning of August nineteenth he broke camp at Dobbs Ferry; and to make certain no deserter or

* Henry P. Johnston: *The Yorktown Campaign and The Surrender of Cornwallis* (New York, 1881), p. 84.

spy carried any other notion to Clinton, the destination of Washington's troops was kept a secret at headquarters. The Americans and French marched through New Jersey in three columns, one swinging through Morristown, Somerset Court House and Princeton, another through Bound Brook to Somerset, and a third through New Brunswick to Trenton. French ovens and warehouses established at Chatham added to the impression of a feint toward Staten Island. Many officers knew not whither they were going, among them Rochambeau's aide, Count Fersen. Speed and deception were Washington's chief weapons now; Clinton might think anything he pleased, for once the columns converged at Princeton and Trenton, the race to Virginia would be in good part run. How well Washington's movements perplexed Clinton emerges in the British general's memoirs:

> If I had as many reasons to believe that Mr. Washington would move his army into Virginia without a covering fleet as I had to think he would not, I could not have prevented his passing the Hudson under the cover of his forts at Verplank's and Stoney Point. Nor (supposing I had boats properly manned) would it have been advisable to have landed at Elizabethtown, in the face of works which he might easily have occupied, as they were only seven miles from his camp at Chatham, without subjecting my army to be beat *en detail.* Nor could I, when informed of

> his march toward the Delaware, have passed an army in time to have made any impression upon him before he had crossed that river.

On the thirtieth of August Washington's army entered Princeton, and on the thirty-first advanced to Trenton; by then Washington and Rochambeau, ahead of the troops, already were receiving a hero's welcome in Philadelphia. On the second of September the first detachment of Continentals marched into Philadelphia with drums and fifes playing and next day Rochambeau led his smartly uniformed French legions into the city. Despite clouds of dust descending everywhere "like a smothering snow-storm" Philadelphians cheered and ladies stood waving from open windows. On the sixth the Americans, pressing onward, came within reach of the Chesapeake at the head of the Elk, and two days later the French joined them. Washington had learned now that De Grasse already had entered the Chesapeake, and the Duke de Lauzun declared that never had he seen a "man so thoroughly and openly delighted." Philip Audibert, the deputy paymaster-general, arrived with "hard money" borrowed from the intendant of the French army and a month's pay went to all troops except those who, "lost to all sense of honour" and lacking "pride in their profession and the love of their country," had in this critical period deserted "the Standard of Freedom." Sensing the high spirits that touched the troops and their commander-in-chief, one observer remarked: "General Washington and the army are gone to take Lord Cornwallis in his mouse-trap."

In mid-August De Grasse was at Cap François (Cape Haytien) on the north coast of Haiti when the frigate *Concorde* overtook him with the communications from Rochambeau. Borrowing three thousand troops under the Marquis St. Simon and fifteen thousand livres at Havana, he started north with twenty-eight sail-of-the-line and six frigates. On the last day of the month he anchored in Lynnhaven Bay off Hampton Roads.

Events quickened in Virginia. Lafayette's chief concern was that Cornwallis must not escape from Yorktown. Joining his troops and those under Wayne with the West Indian forces under St. Simon at Jamestown Island, he threw a strong line across the peninsula at Williamsburg. Apparently Cornwallis believed that sooner or later British naval forces must rescue him and after reconnoitering Lafayette's camp made no effort to break out of his "mouse-trap."

On September fifth, while St. Simon's troops were disembarking at Jamestown Island, the British fleet hove into view. De Grasse slipped his cables and moved out into the open sea with twenty-four ships-of-the-line, seventeen hundred guns and nineteen thousand sailors. Under Rear Admiral Graves the British strength was nineteen ships-of-the-line, fourteen hundred guns, thirteen thousand seamen. The action opened about quarter-past four that afternoon; by half-past six it had ended. The English counted casualties of ninety men killed, two-hundred and forty-six wounded, and sixteen guns dismounted. The French losses certainly were no less. Graves maneuvered his fleet for four days, found that at least two and perhaps three of his ships had been seriously pounded, and disheartened, returned to New York. Gloom suddenly wore many faces inside Yorktown, and Johann Conrad Doehla, a German mercenary employed by the British, confided with a not unreasonable bitterness in his journal for September eleventh:

> The French fleet now stands to the east in a triple line from Cape Henry to Cape Charles except the 4 *men-of-war* that block the channel to our harbour. According to a deserter's report the Marquis de la Fayette and the Prinz von Zweibrucken are now only a mile from us, strongly intrenched, and already working on a *2nd line* [an error, but fear makes any rumor credible].
>
> We get terrible provisions now, putrid ship's meat and wormy biscuits that have spoiled on the ships. Many of the men have taken sick here with dysentery or the bloody flux and with diarrhea. Also the foul fever is spreading, partly on account of the many

hardships from which we have had little rest day or night, and partly on account of the awful food; but mostly, the nitre-bearing water is to blame for it.

Cotton had been blooming when in mid-August Doehla had marched to Yorktown; now the bolls "as large as hen's eggs or chestnuts" had ripened, and gave Doehla at least one cheerful note to add: "We made ourselves coverlets for the beds and couches in our tents where we slept on it, but we had little time for more than that."

"I reached my own Seat at Mount Vernon (distant 120 Miles from the Hd. of Elk) where I staid till the 12th," Washington wrote in his diary for September ninth, giving no clue to the fact that he had last seen his home on May 4, 1775. Next day he wrote a letter to Lafayette:

> We are thus far, my Dear Marquis, on our way to you. The Counte de Rochambeau has just arrived; General Chastellux will [soon] be here & we propose (after resting tomorrow) to be at Fredericksburg on the night of the 12th.—the 13th. we shall reach New Castle & the next day we expect the pleasure of seeing you at your Encampment.
>
> Should there be any danger as we approach you, I shall be obliged if you will send a party of Horse towards New Kent Court House to meet us. With great personal regard & affection, I am, thy Dear Marquis, Your Most Obedt. Servt.
>
> G^{o} Washington.

P.S. I hope you will keep Lord Cornwallis safe, without Provisions or Forage until we arrive. Adieu.

Colonel St. George Tucker, who had described for his wife the unhappy circumstances when in late June Cornwallis had occupied Williamsburg, soon penned another communication in quite a different mood:

I wrote you Yesterday that General *Washington* had not yet arrived. About four o'Clock in the Afternoon his Approach was announced. He had passed our Camp, which is now in the Rear of the whole Army, before we had Time to parade the Militia. The *French* Line had just Time to form. The *Continentals* had more *Leisure*. He approached without any Pomp or Parade, attended only by a few Horsemen and his own Servants. The Count de *Rochambeau* and General *Hand,* with one or two more Officers were with him. I met him as I was endeavoring to get to Camp from Town, in order to parade the Brigade; but he had already passed it. To my great Surprise he recognized my Features and spoke to me immediately by Name. General *Nelson,* the Marquis, etc., rode up immediately after. Never was more Joy painted in any Countenance than theirs. The Marquis rode up with Precipitation, clasped the General in his Arms, and embraced him with an Ardor not easily described. The whole Army and all the Town were presently in Motion. The General, at the Request of the Marquis *de St. Simon,* rode through the *French* Lines. The Troops were paraded for the Pur-

> pose, and cut a most splendid Figure. He then visited the *Continental* Line. As he entered the Camp the Cannon from the Park of Artillery and from every Brigade announced the happy Event. His Train by this Time was much increased; and Men, Women and Children seemed to vie with each other in Demonstrations of Joy and Eagerness to see their beloved Countryman. . . .

Washington's headquarters were at George Wythe's House, and Rochambeau was entertained by Mrs. Peyton Randolph. Tucker could not conceal the hope which permeated Williamsburg: "*Cornwallis* may now tremble for his Fate, for Nothing but some extraordinary Interposition of his Guardian Angels seems capable of saving him and the whole Army from Captivity."

7

"Oh God! It is All Over!"

INSIDE Yorktown redoubts and entrenchments were more relied upon than Cornwallis's guardian angels. Earthworks were strengthened with the lower tiers of guns from warships and frigates. On September fourteenth, the day Washington arrived in Williamsburg, Doehla's journal reported that "all the trees in front of our line have been cut down; and all the roads guarded and fortified with a strong abattis." Two days later Doehla spent the afternoon cutting trees to make palisades "in the entrenchments of our line around our whole camp"; and on the nineteenth, knowing that the "Rebels had moved many troops in jolly boats from Baltimore here up the James River," Doehla noted that "many houses were torn down in the little city of Yorktown because they were a hindrance outside of our lines." Three days later five fireships "prepared with rosin and sulphur" were sent to dispose of the four French warships blockading the channel, but the night was bright with starlight, the French cut anchor and escaped, and all through the day Doehla watched gloomily the fire-ships burning for naught outside the harbor. Another Hessian diarist, Stephen Popp, confessed the fear that had begun to gnaw secretly: "We had to look forward to an attack by the foe daily by land and by sea."

Washington went to see De Grasse aboard the flagship *Ville de Paris,* a magnificent vessel carrying one hundred and twenty guns; because of "hard blowing and contrary Winds" he did not return to Williamsburg until September twenty-second. All except "a few missing Vessels with the Troops from the head of Elk" had arrived. Then on the twenty-eighth Washington's diary recorded memorable events:

> Having debarked all the Troops and their Baggage, Marched and Encamped them in Front of the City [Williamsburg] and having with some difficulty obtained horses and Waggons sufficient to move our field artillery, Intrenching Tools and such other articles as were indispensibly necessary, we commenced our March for the Investiture of the Enemy at York.
>
> The American Continental and French Troops formed one column on the left, the first in advance; the Militia composed the Right column and Marched by way of Harwoods Mill; half a mile beyond the half way H[ous]e. the French and Americans separated, the former continued on the direct Road to York by the Brick House, the latter filed of[f] to the

> right for Murfords bridge [over Skiffe's Creek] where a junction with the Militia was to be made. About Noon the head of each column arrived at its ground and some of the enemy's Picquets were driven in on the left by a Corps of French Troops, advanced for the purpose, which afforded an opportunity for reconnoitering them on their Right. The enemy's Horse on the right were also obliged to retire from the ground they had Encamped on, and from whence they were employed in reconnoitering the right column.
>
> The line being formed, all the Troops, Officers and Men, lay upon their arms during the Night.

Spare and sinewy, the words are like the man, giving the straight facts. Next day Washington moved the Americans more to the right, occupying the east side of Beaver Dam Creek with a marsh in front "about Cannon shot from the enemys lines." His problem was to determine "upon a plan of attack and approach which must be done without the assistance of the Shipping above the Town as the admiral (not withstanding my earnest sollicitation) declined hazarding any Vessels on that Station."

Writing to Clinton that twenty-ninth of September, Cornwallis assumed a bold front, admitting that "I have ventured these last two days to look General Washington's whole force in the face" and assuring Clinton "there was but one wish throughout the whole army, which was, that the enemy would advance." The Hessian, Stephen

Popp, did not sound quite so cheerful: "At night about 1:00 all the regiments moved back to the city, all in silence, because the enemy always came nearer and stronger." Nor did Johann Doehla, who that day helped bury one picket and held down another while a ball was cut from between his shoulder blades: "In our retreat, 3 men from our regiment . . . and 5 men from the Ansbach Regiment deserted."

With the end of September the British, as Popp indicated, withdrew to the inner defenses of Yorktown, and the Allies occupied the abandoned exterior works, finding, in Washington's words, that "with a little alteration" these entrenchments became "very serviceable to us." Thereafter until the sixth of October Washington recorded that "nothing occurred of Importance," which was truly understating the case. Troops thrown across the York River sealed off British entrenchments, redoubts and batteries mounting nineteen guns on Gloucester Point. On Pigeon Hill, two miles southwest of Yorktown, the Allies labored on two enclosed works. Understanding that no siege can have a real bite until the heavy guns are brought up, Washington prodded this activity along the James River. Fascines (fagots used in constructing earthworks) and gabions (bottomless wicker baskets filled with earth or sand) strengthened the lines of the besiegers. Sergeant Joseph Martin, who now had plodded a long way from his native Massachusetts to fight for freedom, recalled a stranger who came

> . . . alone to us, having on a surtout, as we conjectured (it being exceedingly dark), and inquired for the engineers. We now began to be a little jealous of our safety, being alone and without arms and within forty rods of the British trenches. The stranger inquired what troops we were, talked familiarly with us a few minutes, when, being informed which way the officers had gone, he went off in the same direction, after strictly charging us, in case we should be taken prisoners, not to discover to the enemy what troops we were. We were obliged to him for his kind advice, but we considered ourselves as standing in no great need of it. . . .
>
> In a short time, the engineers returned and the aforementioned stranger with them. They discoursed together some time, when by the officers often calling him, "Your Excellency," we discovered that it was General Washington. Had we dared, we might have cautioned him for exposing himself so carelessly to danger at such a time, and doubtless he would have taken it in good part if we had. . . .

Sergeant Martin later described Washington striking "a few blows with a pickaxe, a mere ceremony, that it might be said, 'General Washington with his own hands first broke ground at the siege of Yorktown.' " With fifteen hundred "Fatigue men" digging trenches and twenty-eight hundred covering them, Washington estimated Allied casualties at one French officer and twenty men killed and wounded, declaring that "The work was executed with so much secrecy and dispatch that the enemy were, I believe, totally ignorant of our labor till the light of the Morning discovered it to them."

But as early as October 1 the Hessian Popp had a clear notion of what was afoot: "The enemy began to fortify heavily to really block us up. They threw no shots against us, because they had no cannon yet. . . . We had so much work and annoyance that we had no rest day or night. We were not allowed out at night anymore, because the outposts always came together and every moment there was an alarm." And Johann Doehla, serving picket duty on October 5, drew a picture of what it was like when

> . . . one had either to sit or lie the 2 hours one stood post, so that he could not be seen against the starry sky from the enemy's outposts, which often stood scarcely 5-600 paces distant from us. When it was quiet one could hear every relieving of watch and patrols; and now French, now English or German, calling out: "Who's there?" "Friend!" . . . Throughout the night the location of the post is altered in order that the enemy might observe the less. Everything must proceed quietly. One dares call out neither to sentry nor patrol except to give only the agreed signal. Nor does one dare smoke tobacco nor make a fire. The men call it the "lost post" with all justice.

The first week of October ended without a shot from Allied cannon, though, by Doehla's testimony, the British "fired at them continually this whole time both by day as well as by night, with cannon, bombs, and howitzers." The British took comfort in the belief that Washington had only regimental cannon to turn on them; suddenly, on the ninth of October, they were rudely awakened. About three o'clock that afternoon a French battery opened fire opposite Fusilier's Redoubt on the right wing of the British line; by evening Washington's batteries of the first parallel were pounding the British left. Doehla captured graphically the consternation that smote Yorktown:

> ... They threw bombs in here from 100, 150 pounds and also some of 200 pounds; and their howitzer and cannon balls were of 18, 24, and 36, and very few of 12 pounds. One could therefore not avoid the horribly many cannon balls either inside or outside the city. Most of the inhabitants who were still to be found here fled with their best possessions eastward to the bank of the York River, and dug in among the sand cliffs, but there also they did not stay undamaged; for many were badly injured and mortally wounded by the fragments of bombs which exploded partly in the air and partly on the ground, their arms and legs severed or themselves struck dead. . . .

Colonel Daniel Trabue, who visited Yorktown after the siege, could add further understanding to this danger:

> When a shell fell on the ground it would sink under the ground so Deep that when it burst it would throw up a wagon load, or even more of Dirt; and when it fell on a house it Tore it to pieces. The British had a number of holes and Pits Dug all over the Fort, some large and some small with timber in the top edge; when the soldiers would see a shell coming near them they could jump in one of the pits and squat Down until it had burst. . . . When a shell would fall on any hard place, so that it would not go under the ground, a soldier would go to it, knock off the fiz, or neck, and then it would not burst. The soldier then received a shilling for the act. They said that they did not care much about their life, but the shilling would buy spirits!

Red hot shot from the French battery on the right fired the 44-gun frigate *Charon,* and this blaze spread to two transports. Colonel St. George Tucker repeated the rumor that "Lord Cornwallis has built a kind of Grotto at the foot of the secretary's Garden where he lives under Ground." On October 11, assigned to ship watch along the river, Doehla reported that

> . . . during these 24 hours 3,600 shot were counted from the enemy, which they fired at the town, our line, and at the ships in the harbour. These ships were miserably ruined and shot to pieces. Also the bombs and cannon balls hit many inhabitants and negroes of the city, and marines, sailors, and soldiers. One saw men lying nearly everywhere who were mortally

> wounded and whose heads, arms, and legs had been shot off. Also one saw wounded continually dragged and carried down by the water. Likewise on watch and on post in the lines, on trench and work details, they were wounded by the terribly heavy fire; and soldiers and sailors were always digging in the sand by the water. I saw with astonishment today on my watch how the enemy cannon balls of 24 and more pounds flew over our whole line and the city into the river, where they often struck through 1 and 2 ships, and indeed even struck 10-12 times in the water; yes, some even went clear across the river to Gloucester, where they even injured some soldiers on the beach. I saw bombs fall into the water and lie there for 5, 6-8 and more minutes and then still explode, which was so repulsive and horrible in the water that one can scarcely believe it. It showered upon the river bank the sand and mud from below; if one sat there, it felt like the shocks of an earthquake.

The Allied cannon, Washington admitted, "did much execution," and well they might, Doehla would have testified, holding "a piece of an exploded bomb in my hands which weighed more than 30 pounds and was over 3 inches thick." With Teutonic thoroughness Doehla detailed every leg or arm he saw severed; the poor devils in the light infantry who had to stand in the fore-bastion, called a hornwork, took the bitterest punishment, according to Popp.

A glance at a map of the battlefield at Yorktown reveals the irresistible logic, and the devastating, evermounting pressure that Washington exerted on Cornwallis. Washington's army numbered about 16,000, that of Cornwallis about 7,500. Washington's force was deployed in a semi-circle around the British, with the intention of squeezing his foe into submission. Basic to a successful siege, such as that at Yorktown, was a series of long trenches (called parallels) that covered the troops supporting the batteries of attacking artillery. The bombardment that stunned Yorktown, beginning on the ninth of October, was fired from the batteries of the first parallel. Meanwhile the Allies dug steadily on a second parallel, and by the morning of the twelfth, Colonel Tucker said, these trenches were "within two hundred yards in some points of the Enemies Works." Alert to the danger next day British cannoneers pounded the Allies with a grim determination, bringing into action effective, destructive mortars called "royals"; yet, cheerfully, Washington began his diary for October 14: "The day was spent in compleating our parallel, and maturing the Batteries of the second parallel."

Actually the Allies approached two advanced British redoubts, called Numbers Nine and Ten, which with fraise work, moats and abatis blocked the Allied approach to the shore. The fourteenth of October was a Sunday, and toward seven o'clock Doehla found "a thick fog" over the field. At Redoubt Number Ten a Hessian picket, hearing a movement in the misty night, cried: *"Wer da?"* When there was no answer, a warning shot was fired. Out of the darkness and into the ditch beneath the fraise work charged French troops under Count Guillaume de Deux-Ponts. The French grenadiers, declared Doehla, came with "long storming pikes, assaulted with the greatest agility, sprang into the moat, tore away the stakes"—a spirited picture, to which Deux-Ponts added: "The enemy kept up a sharp fire and charged us at the point of bayonet, but no one was driven back."

If subsequent accounts are confused, so was the action itself. Doehla thought three thousand French and Americans made the assault, which was stretching the figure, since four hundred grenadiers under Deux-Ponts attacked Redoubt Nine and an equal number of Americans under Colonel Alexander Hamilton assaulted Redoubt Ten. Yet one can credit Doehla's assertion that "they made such a terrible yell and loud cheering that one believed nothing but that the whole 'Wild Hunt' had broken out." Among the Americans was that redoubtable son of Massachusetts, Sergeant Joseph Martin, grinning to himself as his friends tried to pronounce the watchword "Rochambeau" and said instead a plain Yankee "Rush, on boys" that served equally well. As the British opened a sharp fire, Martin remembered

> . . . We were now at a place where many of our large shells had burst in the ground, making holes sufficient to bury an ox in. The men, having their eyes fixed upon what was transacting before them, were every now and then falling into these holes. I thought the British were killing us off at a great rate. At length, one of the holes happening to pick me up, I found out the mystery of the huge slaughter.
>
> As soon as the firing began, our people began to cry, "The fort's our own!" and it was "Rush on, boys!" The sappers and miners soon cleared a passage for the infantry who entered it rapidly. Our miners were ordered not to enter the fort, but there was no stopping them. "We will go," said they. "Then go to the d—l," said the commanding officer of our corps, "if you will."

Doehla, not hiding his pique, complained of a strategem:

> . . . at the center of our line one heard loud commands given in German—"The whole column or brigade forward march! Halt! Cannons to the front!" and that two or three times; also some bullets flew over the ramparts in the center of our line. Thereby they made a false alarm and made us believe they would attack us in the center.

As a result, Doehla grumbled, they "luckily took the 2 redoubts." Colonel Deux-Ponts, on the point of leaping into the redoubt and charging the enemy with bayonets, commented with Gallic frugality: "Then they laid down their arms and we leaped with more tranquility and less risk," which was undoubtedly true. *"Vive le Roi!"* shouted Deux-Ponts, grenadiers, chausseurs, the troops in the trenches—"to which the enemy replied by a general discharge of artillery and musketry." Now, said Deux-Ponts, "I never saw a sight more beautiful or more majestic." The Baron de Viomenil warned Deux-Ponts to prepare for a vigorous defense, and, added Deux-Ponts, not above sprinkling salt in an open wound, "the Baron . . . judged the English general by himself." Yet Sergeant Martin did not disparage the quality of the British defense: "As I mounted the breastwork, I met an old associate hitching himself down into the trench. I knew him by the light of the enemy's musketry, it was so vivid." The forts were taken; the fog in early evening turned to rain, but the Allies toiled the night through in the mud making the captured forts part of the second parallel. A soggy morning found Cornwallis advising Clinton: "We shall soon be exposed to an assault in ruined works, in a bad position, and with weakened numbers. The safety of the place is, therefore, so precarious that I cannot recommend that the fleet and army should run great risk in endeavoring to save us."

To this point Washington reckoned that the siege of Yorktown had cost two officers killed and seven wounded, fifty soldiers killed and one hundred and twenty-seven wounded.

The fifteenth of October saw two howitzers placed in each of the captured redoubts and at about five o'clock that afternoon these weapons began pounding the British. "But we didn't owe them any shots," commented the Hessian Popp with a flash of spirit. Yet the breaking point approached. At daybreak on the sixteenth three hundred and fifty British under Lieutenant Colonel Abercrombie launched a sortie against two batteries in the center of the second parallel; Doehla reported that, falling upon the Allies in a trench, the British "bayonetted many and spiked in a hurry 11 of their guns" but the detachment "returned very quickly in good order with unimportant losses." That afternoon, Doehla thought, "the enemy cannonaded terribly." Cornwallis could no longer deny the horns of his dilemma, writing Clinton that his choice was either "preparing to surrender the next day, or endeavouring to get off with the greatest part of the troops."

Cornwallis planned carefully. Sixteen large boats would ferry his infantry across the York to Gloucester that night, leaving no more than a token force inside Yorktown to surrender the city for the sick, the wounded, and the unhappy civilians. The American and French forces sealing off Gloucester posed no real obstacle to Cornwallis; under pressure he should effect a quick breakthrough into Maryland and be on his way by rapid marches to join Clinton in New York.

The operation across the York began, a small portion of Cornwallis's troops reached Gloucester, then the unpredictible Chesapeake produced a violent windstorm. Boats were swept helplessly down river. The force already transported to Gloucester could not be moved back. Cornwallis and his army were hung like an ox over a fence. In the second parallel Washington's batteries opened at daybreak, certainly no solace to the harried British who now seemed to be contending with God as well as the Allies. By daylight Cornwallis finally succeeded in rowing his troops back from Gloucester.

A dejected Cornwallis tried to explain his plight in a letter to Clinton. Washington's cannon had left his works in ruins—he could not argue that point with his engineer and principal officers. He "could not fire a single gun" and had but "one eight-inch and little more than a hundred cohorn shells"; moreover, "a diversion by the French ships of war that lay at the mouth of York River was to be expected." Sickness and fatigue had weakened his troops where the enemy had not. Gloomily he faced reality: "It would have been wanton and inhuman to the last degree to sacrifice the lives of this small body of gallant soldiers, who had ever behaved with so much fidelity and courage, by exposing them to an assault, which from the numbers and precaution of the enemy, could not fail to succeed."

Obviously Cornwallis expected that in a day or so, even within hours, the Allies would storm the town. On October 16, in much the same vein, the laconic Stephen Popp observed: "In the morning the enemy came so close to the horn works with a trench and battery of 14 cannon there was hardly a stone's throw separating. Yes, their approach was so advantageous that if we could hold out a few days longer, they could come right into our hideout." Now, on the seventeenth, Johann Doehla found the morning opening "even more horribly than ever before" and standing in the hornworks Doehla "saw nothing but bombs and balls raining on our whole line." Cornwallis came in person to inspect the hornworks where Doehla waited. He accepted the inevitable.

At ten o'clock a drummer mounted the British parapet and beat a parley. At once an officer appeared outside the works, holding up a white handkerchief. Still beating, the drummer stepped to the officer's side. And Ebenezer Denny, who had fought his way out of Cornwallis's trap at Green Spring, recorded the scene to which the road since then had led: "Our batteries ceased. An officer from our lines ran and met the other and tied the handkerchief over his eyes. The drummer [was] sent back, and the British officer conducted to a house in the rear of our lines. Firing ceased totally." Cornwallis proposed a truce of twenty-four hours for drawing up terms of surrender.

"To this he was answered," Washington wrote in his diary for October seventeenth, "that a desire to spare the further effusion of Blood would readily incline me to treat of the surrender of the above Posts [Yorktown and Gloucester], but previous to the meeting of Commissioners I wished to have his proposals in writing and for this purpose would grant a cessation of hostilities two hours."

The surrender negotiations proved nettlesome to both sides. In suggesting that British troops be allowed to return to England and German troops to Germany under parole not to serve again during the war, Cornwallis proposed terms such as Burgoyne had offered and Gates had accepted in 1777. To Washington such terms were "inadmissible"; and his own proposals followed the terms imposed by the British upon the Americans at Charleston. The meeting of the commissioners next day at Augustine Moore's farmhouse had its hot-tempered moments. The Americans insisted that "the troops shall march out with colors cased and drums beating a British or a German march." Cornwallis's aide called the article "harsh," and was reminded that at Charleston after a brave defense of six weeks the Americans had been required to march out with colors cased and drums "*not* beating a German or British march." The stiff British reply: "My Lord Cornwallis did not command at Charleston." The stiff American rejoinder: "It is not the individual that is concerned here. It is the nation."

The men in the hornworks left the bickering to the commissioners. "We were heartily glad that it should finally come to an end," confessed Stephen Popp, who recounted how, on the evening of the seventeenth, "a tragic accident occurred very suddenly":

> . . . about 7:00 one of our powder magazines went off. The circumstances are these: The English cannoneers were inside and had orders to fill the bombs and howitzers with powder. Those same cannoneers with their conscripts were intoxicated with brandy. So it was suspected that they had not been careful with the light and the magazine went off. It killed 13 persons, some of whom were blasted to bits, others terribly crushed and buried in dirt. Among them was an Ansbach grenadier who stood guard there and lost his life. Of him only a coat plait and a piece of his pocket braid were found. Of others we found only pieces of bodies and limbs.

At dawn next morning Colonel St. George Tucker listened as "the British gave us a serenade with the Bag pipe, I believe, & were answered by the French." As the sun rose, Colonel Tucker beheld one of "the most striking pictures" of the war: "From the point of Rock Battery on one side our Lines compleatly mann'd and our Works crowded with soldiers were exhibited to view—opposite these at the Distance of two hundred yards you were presented with a sight of the British Works, their parapets crowded with officers looking at those who were assembled at the top of our Works." On the beach "hundreds of busy people might be seen moving to & fro"; ships were "sunk down to the Waters Edge" and in the channel "the Masts, Yards & even the top gallant Masts of some might be seen, without any vestige of the hulls." Across the York loomed the fortifications on Gloucester, and distantly two French ships of war moved under sail. "A painter need not to have wish'd for a more compleat subject to imploy his pencil without any experience of Genius," thought Tucker, on this day "when the pride of Britain was to be humbled."

Throughout the eighteenth flags of truce kept passing between the lines; the discussions at the Moore House were hammered through to points of hard-headed agreement; then the truce was extended until nine o'clock the following morning. At noon Washington signed the terms "in the trenches before Yorktown, in Virginia, October 19, 1781," and detachments of French and Americans began taking possession of the British forts. After numerous delays, this same day Clinton sailed from New York to rescue Cornwallis; a British fleet of twenty-five sail-of-the-line and ten frigates would carry about seven thousand English and German troops to the approaches to Chesapeake Bay before on the twenty-fourth of October Clinton learned that Cornwallis had surrendered.

At two o'clock on the afternoon of October nineteenth

Washington mounted his white charger and rode to the field for the formal surrender. The sun shone warmly. In sparkling uniforms the French legions formed behind the beaming Rochambeau, the happy Lafayette. Shoulder to shoulder stood the men and officers of Massachusetts and Virginia, of Pennsylvania and the Carolinas, of New Hampshire, New York, New Jersey and Maryland—seasoned comrades now who had marched far and fought long for this moment when down the road came the doleful British with fifes playing and drums beating. One American thought critically that "the British prisoners appeared much in liquor"; and another contended that "the British officers in general behaved like boys who had been whipped at school. Some bit their lips, some pouted, others cried." All eyes, said Lieutenant Colonel Harry Lee, searched for the British commander-in-chief, "anxious to look at the man, heretofore so much the object of their dread," but "Cornwallis held himself back from the humiliating scene; obeying sensations which his great character ought to have stifled." Colonel Fontaine of the Virginia Militia declared that British "knees seemed to tremble"; and felt compelled to speak a loyal word for the French, who were "very different from the ideas formerly inculcated in us, of a people living on frogs & coarse vegetables."

It was about three o'clock when the defeated army appeared, and with them was Johann Doehla, who, having been paid to take his chances come what may, accepted his fate in good spirit:

> We marched out Williams Street, or down the road which leads to Williamsburg, in column with shouldered muskets, through the whole enemy army, with our drummers beating a march. The entire army of the allied force, French and Americans, stood by regiments under arms *en parade;* in front of these regiments were the generals and staff officers . . .
>
> On the right flank, every regiment of the French paraded white silk colors adorned with 3 silver lilies; beyond the colors stood drummers and fifers and in front of the colors the *Haubisten* [band] which made splendid music. In general the French troops appeared very well, they were good-looking, tall, well-washed men. All wore white gaiters; the facings of some of the regiments were red, most were white, and some green. The German Alsace Regiment was clothed in blue. To our left as we marched out, or on the left flank, stood the American troops drawn up on parade with their generals, Washington, Gates, and Wayne. They stood in 3 ranks, first the regular troops which also had *Haubisten* and musicians making beautiful music and appeared tolerable enough. After them were the militia from Virginia and Maryland who looked rather badly tattered and torn.

Along the same road marched Stephen Popp, and he also believed that

. . . the Virginia Militia, . . couldn't hold a candle to the first ones . . . We observed all these troops with amazement and were staggered by the multitude of them who had besieged us. We appreciated also at the same time that we were just a guard-mounting in comparison . . and that they could have eaten us up with their power. . . .

After we had marched through both armies we came to a level place, where the Hussars of the French were drawn up in a circle, where we and all the regiment of Lord Cornwallis' army—Alas!—laid down our weapons and armor. . . .

Doehla, hearing the command to "Ground arms and take off cartridge-boxes and sabers," admitted his "tears." In silence the defeated soldiers marched back to their camp with "nothing more than our few effects in the packs on our backs," and with understandable bitterness Doehla remarked upon "the Americans" who "greatly jeered at us like conquerors," adding:

In general the French conducted themselves very well toward us, but of the Americans—except for the officers—none were permitted in the city or in our lines, for the French grenadiers had strongly surrounded all our works and also Yorktown and allowed no one inside, because they feared the American militia—which is never far from stealing—might also steal from us and plunder us, or otherwise make mischief according to their custom.

The old German watchman who awakened Philadelphians by crying "Basht dree o'glock, und Cornval-lis isht da-ken!" symbolized the joy that swept the country with the news of the surrender at Yorktown. Lord Wraxall described the scene when in London the same intelligence reached Lord North: "I asked Lord George afterwards, how he took the Communication, when made to him? 'As he would have taken a Ball in his Breast,' replied Lord George. For, he opened his Arms, exclaiming wildly, as he paced up and down the Apartment during a few Minutes, 'Oh God! it is all over!' Words which he repeated many Times, under Emotions of the deepest consternation and Distress." A message was dispatched to the King at Kew, "acquainting him with the melancholy Termination of Lord Cornwallis's Expedition," and the reminiscences of Lord Wraxall continued:

> . . . it was impossible for all present not to feel a lively Curiosity to know how the King had received the Intelligence; as well as how he had expressed himself in his Note to Lord George Germain, on the first Communication of so painful an Event. He gratified our Wish by reading it to us; observing at the same Time, that it did the highest Honor to His Majesty's Fortitude, Firmness, and Consistency of Character. . . . The Billet ran nearly to this Effect: "I have received with Sentiments of the deepest Concern, the Communication which Lord George Germain has made me, of the unfortunate Result of the

> Operations in Virginia. I particularly lament it, on Account of the Consequences connected with it, and the Difficulties which it may produce in carrying on the public Business, or in repairing such a Misfortune. But, I trust that neither Lord George Germain, nor any Member of the Cabinet will suppose, that it makes the smallest Alteration in those Principles of my Conduct, which have directed me in past Time, and which will always continue to animate me under every Event, in the Prosecution of the present Contest."

For himself Wraxall commented: "Whatever Opinion we may entertain, relative to the Practicability of reducing America to Obedience by Force of Arms, at the End of 1781; we must admit, that no Sovereign could manifest more Calmness, Dignity, or Self-Command, than George the Third displayed in this Reply."

So at last had the pieces fallen into place to fashion the majestic mosaic of Yorktown. Wethersfield, Dobbs Ferry, New Jersey, Philadelphia, the Head of Elk, Mount Vernon, Williamsburg . . . these marked the brilliant pattern Washington had given to a masterpiece. The Carolinas, the Appomattox, Richmond, Williamsburg, Jamestown, Portsmouth, Yorktown . . . these were the pieces of the aging Cornwallis and the youthful Lafayette as they played their game of hound and hare across Virginia. And Newport, Cap François, Capes Charles and Henry at the entrance to Chesapeake Bay . . . here the bold border around the mosaic was formed. Failure of the British campaigns in the North had produced the campaigns in the South, but now these too had been crushed, so that Yorktown became the crippling blow from which England never would recover. Washington, with that simple wholeness that spelled his greatness, ended his order of congratulations to the Allied army: "Divine service is to be performed tomorrow in the several brigades and divisions. The Commander in Chief earnestly recommends that the troops not on duty should universally attend with that seriousness of Deportment and gratitude of Heart which the recognition of such reiterated and astonishing interpositions of Providence demand of us."

A beautiful autumn lingered along the peninsula of Virginia in 1781. Geese honked above the marshes that surrounded Jamestown Island, where on a spring day one hundred and seventy-four years before Englishmen had come to seek a fortune and had stayed in the face of incredible hardships to build an empire. Along Duke of Gloucester Street in Williamsburg the foliage of the trees turned a deep yellow, a bright russet—and a serenity came to this grand old thoroughfare where in ten turbulent years the Revolution became a victory in mind and heart before the first gun was fired. And at Yorktown, on bluffs that looked over calm waters now, the stars shone brightly upon the scarred fields of battle where the strength of Washington had finally prevailed.

The distance from Jamestown to Yorktown may be traveled in minutes. The restored buildings and fortifications are there to see. And there for the heart to feel and the mind to know is the spirit of the people who built these monuments by living from day to day in a homeland that became very dear to them.

A Bibliographical Note and Index

A Bibliographical Note

I. JAMESTOWN: Doorway to Empire

No modern student of the early years at Jamestown escapes a lasting indebtedness to Lyon Gardiner Tyler for his splendid editing of *Narratives of Early Virginia, 1606-1625* (New York, 1907). From this volume are drawn the original texts by George Percy, John Smith, Don Diego de Molina, John Rolfe, and the Proceedings of the Virginia Assembly for 1619, as here quoted. The source for the quotation from *Eastward Ho!* is Philip A. Bruce's *Economic History of Virginia in the Seventeenth Century* (New York, 2 vols., 1896); and Smith's account of his early career is drawn from *The True Travels, Adventures, and Observations of Captaine John Smith* (New York, 1930). Samuel H. Yonge's *The Site of Old "James Towne," 1607-1698* (Richmond, 1936) and Henry Chandlee Forman's *Jamestown and St. Mary's: Buried Cities of Romance* (Baltimore, 1938) provide useful insight into the settlement and its people; and *Records of the Virginia Company of London,* edited by Susan Myra Kingsbury (Washington, 1906-35) and *Journals of the House of Burgesses of Virginia,* edited by H. R. McIlwaine (Richmond, 1909), are other sources reflected in these pages. For general background of the early colonial period, layman and scholar must admire Louis B. Wright's *The Atlantic Frontier* (New York, 1947); even though one may not agree entirely with the conclusions of Thomas J.

Wertenbaker's *Torchbearer of the Revolution* (Princeton, 1940), it remains a volume of great knowledge concerning the personalities and events behind Bacon's Rebellion; and for this author at least passing decades do not dim either the literary charm or the lively viewpoints of John Fiske in his *Old Virginia and Her Neighbors* (Boston and New York, 2 vols., 1897).

II. WILLIAMSBURG: Cradle of Revolution

The files of special material supplied by Colonial Williamsburg, Inc. when I worked on *Rebel's Roost* (Williamsburg, 1956) were again of invaluable assistance in writing these chapters. Among published sources used that promise the general reader hours of pleasure and profit, a special word must be spoken for Rutherfoord Goowin's *A Brief and True Report Concerning Williamsburg in Virginia* (Williamsburg, 1941), Carl Bridenbaugh's *Seat of Empire* (Williamsburg, 1950), and Charles S. Sydnor's *Gentlemen Freeholders* (Chapel Hill, 1952). *The Diaries of George Washington,* 1748-1799, edited by John C. Fitzpatrick (Boston and New York, 1925) and *The Writings of George Washington,* edited by John C. Fitzpatrick (Washington, 1931-44) were used; and also *The Papers of Thomas Jefferson,* edited by Julian P. Boyd, Lyman H. Butterfield and Mina R. Bryan (Princeton, 1950—). Helen Hill [Miller]: *George Mason: Constitu-*

tionalist (Cambridge, 1938) proved a useful volume; and both Dumas Malone: *Jefferson the Virginian: Jefferson and His Time* (Boston, I, 1948) and Douglas Southall Freeman: *George Washington* (New York, 1948-54) hold rich interest for those attracted to this period.

III. YORKTOWN: Triumph of Faith

A special word of gratitude belongs to Edward Miles Riley for making available a copy of "The Founding and Development of Yorktown, Virginia, 1691-1781," (Ph.D. Thesis, University of Southern California, 1942). Likewise of great help was Charles E. Hatch, Jr.'s "The 'Affair Near James Island' (or, 'The Battle of Green Spring') July 6, 1781," *Virginia Magazine of History and Biography,* LIII (1945), 172-196. "The Doehla Journal," translated by Robert J. Tilden, appears in the *William and Mary Quarterly,* 2d ser., XXII (1942); *A Hessian Soldier in the American Revolution: The Diary of Stephen Popp,* translated by Reinhart J. Pope was privately printed (N.P.: 1953); and "St. George Tucker's Journal of the Siege of Yorktown, 1781," edited by Edward M. Riley, appears in the *William and Mary Quarterly,* 3d ser., V (1948). For general background on these events a fine work is Henry P. Johnston's *The Yorktown Campaign and The Surrender of Cornwallis* (New York, 1881); there is much good material on Yorktown in Henry B. Carrington's *Battles of the American Revolution* (New York, 1876); and yet for both a lively and reliable telling of the Yorktown campaign—indeed, of the entire war—an unexcelled work is *Rebels and Redcoats* by George F. Scheer and Hugh F. Rankin (New York, 1957).

So, in conclusion, I list, as Charles Reade once said, some of the cows I have milked; but insist, as he insisted, that the cheese must remain my own.

Index

BLOOD OF FREEDOM

was composed and printed by the William Byrd Press, Inc., in 1958 for Colonial Williamsburg, Williamsburg, Virginia. The types used are Granjon and Caslon 337. The paper is Perkins & Squier Antique Wove made by the Glatfelter Paper Company. Binding was by the Russell Rutter Company, Inc., New York. The book was designed by John J. Walklet, Jr. Maps and illustrations by Richard J. Stinely.